BECOMING
EUROPEAN

BECOMING EUROPEAN

Challenges for Georgia in the Twenty-First Century

Vladimer Papava

iUniverse

BECOMING EUROPEAN
CHALLENGES FOR GEORGIA IN THE
TWENTY-FIRST CENTURY

Copyright © 2021 Vladimer Papava.

All rights reserved. No part of this book may be used or reproduced by any means, graphic, electronic, or mechanical, including photocopying, recording, taping or by any information storage retrieval system without the written permission of the author except in the case of brief quotations embodied in critical articles and reviews.

iUniverse books may be ordered through booksellers or by contacting:

iUniverse
1663 Liberty Drive
Bloomington, IN 47403
www.iuniverse.com
844-349-9409

Because of the dynamic nature of the Internet, any web addresses or links contained in this book may have changed since publication and may no longer be valid. The views expressed in this work are solely those of the author and do not necessarily reflect the views of the publisher, and the publisher hereby disclaims any responsibility for them.

Any people depicted in stock imagery provided by Getty Images are models, and such images are being used for illustrative purposes only. Certain stock imagery © Getty Images.

ISBN: 978-1-6632-0762-3 (sc)
ISBN: 978-1-6632-0763-0 (e)

Library of Congress Control Number: 2020924604

Print information available on the last page.

iUniverse rev. date: 12/28/2020

PRAISE FOR
BECOMING EUROPEAN

"Former Economy Minister and Professor Vladimer Papava offers a collection of telling essays of Georgia in transition with a dream of Europe under illiberal pressure from Russia, but most of all facing up to the domestic political reality. These highly-readable essays tell us how difficult it is to be between everything and to try to get it right. The reader is left with a strong sense of instability but also capture."

—ANDERS ÅSLUND, Senior Fellow, Atlantic Council, and Adjunct Professor, Georgetown University, USA

"This volume is the most comprehensive and insightful volume written on Georgia's transition from a Soviet republic to an independent country with a market-based economy. This compilation of essays tracks the evolution of economics, politics, and foreign policy in Georgia and in its neighbors, especially in Russia. The volume dissects the problems that have accompanied this transition over the past three decades.

The author, Professor Vladimer Papava, provides a trenchant, in-depth analysis of the ways in which Georgian policy is often superficial: changes in economic policy that are presumed to be major often mask the lack of change in how Georgian government officials operate and in the structure of the economy. The essays also highlight the importance of the European Union and the United States in supporting Georgia and encouraging change. Of particular note is the historical nature of the collection; one can savor how the author analyzed events at major junctures in recent Georgian history. This book is to be recommended for those individuals interested in the course of the transition, especially in the former Soviet republics of the Caucasus and Central Asia."

—KEITH W. CRANE, Senior Fellow, Science and Technology Policy Institute, Washington, DC, USA

"No country in this century has had a more complicated geopolitical fate than the Republic of Georgia, and no analyst has provided greater insights on the twists and turns Tbilisi has gone through over that period that Vladimer Papava. His new collection of essays he has written over the last 15 years will solidify his reputation as the indispensable guide to Georgia and its relations with the world."

—PAUL GOBLE, Former Special Advisor on Soviet Nationalities at the US Department of State, and Adjunct Professor, Institute of World Politics, USA

"Professor Papava has assembled here an interesting and useful collection of notes and papers on the evolution of economic policy in Georgia. The story starts with the Rose Revolution of 2003, moving on to the Russian invasion of 2008, and the linked notion of Russia's "liberal" empire; then the financial crisis, and moves towards the EU. There is much discussion of alternative economic models for Georgia, various policy mistakes, and thoughts on how to manage the economy better. The volume ends with some recent thoughts on our latest problem, the COVID-19 pandemic. Overall, a nice volume, a good introduction to the Georgian economy, and it deserves to be widely read."

—PAUL HARE, Professor Emeritus, Heriot-Watt University, Edinburgh, Scotland, UK

"Vladimer Papava has put together an eclectic collection of articles which examines Georgia's struggle for democratic and economic modernization over the last two decades. Papava is one of the finest and most critical economists in Georgia, and in this volume provides us with a wide-ranging analysis of the economic, social and foreign policies of Georgia since 2000. He writes honestly about the outcomes of the Rose Revolution and the rise of shadow politics under Bidzina Ivanishvili. He examines Georgia's relations with Russia, China, and the EU, and explores the region's energy politics. Papava's evaluation of the country's economic options, and his discussion of potential models and scenarios, reminds us why Georgia needs home-grown economists and specialists who have an intimate knowledge of the country along with an independent and critical perspective."

—STEPHEN F. JONES, Professor, Russian and Eurasian Studies/International Relations, Mount Holyoke College, USA

"This compilation of short articles written over a substantial period of Georgia's post-USSR independence provides a very useful tour d'horizon of the challenges facing Georgia in economic policy, politics, and international relations. The book provides valuable insight into Georgia's evolution, Russia's challenge, and Western ambivalence. It draws together pipeline policy through the evolution of economic regionalism to regional perspectives on East-West relations. Well worth reading."

—NEIL MACFARLANE, Professor, Oxford University, Oxford, UK

"This compendium of online commentary on Georgia's politics and economics over the past fiveteen years (since 2006) will give the non-specialist reader a detailed introduction to this small Caucasus country's tribulations and hopes. A distinguished economist/scholar and former Minister of the Economy, Papava is unsparing in his analyses of Georgia's economic policies under both Saakashvili and his Georgian Dream successors, and of Russia's predations along its southern borders under Putin. A taste of everyday realities at a world crossroads."

> —THOMAS W. SIMONS, Jr., former U.S. Ambassador to Poland and Pakistan, Visiting Scholar, Davis Center for Russian and Eurasian Studies, Harvard University, USA

"Vladimer Papava's "Becoming European: Challenges for Georgia in the Twenty-First Century" is a tour de force, in at least four dimensions. First, it offers a compelling account of Georgia's economics, political economy, and external relations during the past two decades. Second, it is a book of reflections of a former Minister of Economy on the real-world policy challenges faced by a developing country that both belongs to, and whose orientation is contested by, both Europe and Eurasia. Third, it an expert account of a national transition away from Soviet-type socialism to market capitalism—with all the challenges and compromises that such transitions necessarily entail. And finally, it is a forward-looking attempt to map Georgia's past and present against the emerging economic challenges of the 21st century. As such, this book is a must read for anyone seeking broader and deeper understandings of Georgia's development dynamics and their future implications."

> —BEN SLAY, Senior Economist, UNDP Regional Bureau for Europe and CIS

To Lukas Rey

CONTENTS

Preface xvii

1. Russia's Economic Imperialism 1
2. Russia's Illiberal "Liberal Empire" 5
3. Georgia's Hollow Revolution 9
4. Pipeline Harmonization
   Instead of Alternative Pipelines: Why the
   Pipeline "Cold War" Needs to End 23
5. Central Caucaso-Asia: Toward a Redefinition of
   Post-Soviet Central Eurasia 27
6. Russia: Being in the Kremlin Means Never
   Letting Go 32
7. Georgia's "Green Friday" 35
8. Postwar Georgia's Economic Challenges 42
9. Postwar Georgia Pondering New Models of
   Development 49
10. The New Threats of the Old Cold War 56
11. Georgian Economy: Mistakes, Threats, and
    Resolutions 64

12. Postwar Georgia: Current Developments and
    Challenges Ahead.. 85
13. Myths about the Georgian Economy 102
14. Russia's Accession to the WTO: The Perspective
    from Tbilisi 109
15. Democracy: A Goal or Merely a Commitment
    for the West? 118
16. The Kremlin and Georgia: Collusion or Illusion? 124
17. US Elections: Hopes and Expectations from a
    'Post-Rosy' Georgia 132
18. Georgia's Socioeconomic Development:
    Prospects over the Medium Term 138
19. The Georgian Model of Libertarianism and Its
    Applicability to Ukraine 151
20. Economic Models of Eurasianism and the
    Eurasian Union: Why the Future is Not
    Optimistic.. 157
21. For Georgia, GEENTRANCE is Coming!................ 163
22. Post-Communist Georgia Between Two
    Alternatives: EU and the EAEU 168
23. Georgia's Modern Decisions and Threats of
    Expansion of Russian Presence in Caucasus............ 173
24. Primitivism as a Trait of Georgia's Modern
    Economic Policy 179
25. Features of Governmental "Business" in Post-
    Soviet Georgia... 187
26. Belt and Road Initiative, the Russian Factor, and
    Main Challenges for Georgia................................... 191

27. Georgia's Economy in a Tourist Trap.......................... 196
28. Depreciation of the Georgian National
    Currency: Economic, Psychological,
    Administrative, and Political Factors 202
29. Why Georgia Needs Economists............................... 209
30. Why the Population of Georgia Does Not
    Perceive Economic Growth Positively.................... 216
31. Whither Economic Policy?.. 222
32. Moscow's Political Trap for Georgia: Stable
    Instability.. 231
33. Coronomic Crisis: When the Economy is a
    Hostage to Medicine 240
34. Pensions, Economic Growth, Agflation, and
    Inflation 246
35. Georgia's European Way During the Period of
    Pandemic Deglobalization...................................... 254

Index... 265

PREFACE

This book is a collection of electronic publications (blogs, op-eds, policy briefs, and posts) published over the past fifteen years. These articles are devoted to the political and economic problems of post-Communist Georgia in the twenty-first century.

After the collapse of the Soviet Union, post-Soviet countries faced the task of strengthening their state independence. The question of the international orientation of these countries was no less acute. Some post-Soviet countries preferred to remain in the geopolitical orbit of Russia, while others from the very beginning of their state independence were focused on the Euro-Atlantic vector of development.

For Georgia, even before the collapse of the USSR, and especially in the last years of its existence, the priority was a Euro-Atlantic orientation. For some time, Georgia had to be part of the Commonwealth of Independent States (CIS) for political reasons, but after a five-day war with Russia in August 2008, Georgia left the Commonwealth.

Georgia's European path of development has not been an easy one. The formation of a European state in post-Communist

Georgia is associated with many difficult tasks, the solution of which is of paramount importance for the future of this country.

For the comprehensive development of Georgia, the main obstacle remains the occupation and annexation by Russia of Abkhazia and South Ossetia, which in total make up 20 percent of Georgia's territory. Despite this, the continuation of decisive reforms to become closer to the European Union (EU) is excessively important for Georgia.

It should be noted that Georgia has achieved some success on the road to its rapprochement with the EU. On June 27, 2014, the EU-Georgia Association Agreement (AA) was signed in Brussels; it has been in effect since July 1, 2016. The agreement introduces a preferential trade regime: the Deep and Comprehensive Free Trade Area (DCFTA). On February 27, 2017, the EU adopted a regulation on visa liberalization for Georgians traveling to the EU. These agreements opened up new opportunities for Georgia to integrate into the EU. At the same time, Georgia still needs to do a lot of work for a real rapprochement with the EU, and this will require many years of hard work.

It must be emphasized that the EU itself is going through difficult times, especially against the background of Brexit. For its part, too, the COVID-19 pandemic has exposed many of the EU's weaknesses. Despite these difficulties, the new challenges facing the EU should help in finding ways to solve the problems for its further development. All this notwithstanding, the European standards of state-building, democracy, and a market economy do not lose their relevance and importance for Georgia.

Compiling a collection of articles published previously online is a worthwhile undertaking, because each reflects the author's understanding of a particular issue that corresponds to the time of the writing of each piece. It will be useful for the reader to have these articles in one book that reflects the dynamics of the development of the situation in and around Georgia. The footnote of each article gives the full reference of the original online publication.

Some articles published online contain references in the form of relevant links. For the publication of these articles as a part of this book, all the references have been transformed and are presented in written form.

I hope that this book will be interesting for readers trying to understand not only the challenges and problems ahead for Georgia but also the regional and international aspects of the geopolitical and geo-economic situation in the Caucasus in general.

Russia's Economic Imperialism

with S. Frederic Starr

January 17, 2006[*]

Russia's use of natural gas to exert economic and political pressure on Ukraine has caused grave concern in the West. But Russia's pressure on Georgia has been even heavier—and it has scarcely been noticed.

In Georgia, as in Ukraine, Russian President Vladimir Putin seeks to implement the doctrine of a "liberal empire" put forward in October 2003 by Anatoli Chubais, chairman of United Energy System (RAO UES), Russia's energy monopoly. According to Chubais, Russia will never find a place in either NATO or the European Union, so it must create an alternative to both—a new empire of its own. It can do this

---

[*] V. Papava and F. Starr, "Russia's Economic Imperialism," *Project Syndicate*, January 17, 2006, https://www.project-syndicate.org/commentary/russia-s-economic-imperialism.

by using its huge and rich public-private monopolies to take over the key industries and economic institutions of former Soviet republics, thereby laying the groundwork for political domination. The resulting empire will be liberal, according to Chubais's definition, because it can be built with money rather than tanks.

Russia's first step in fulfilling this plan in the South Caucasus was directed against Armenia, its strategic partner in the region. Seizing on a $93 million debt that Armenia owed to Russia, the Putin administration demanded payment in either cash or equity in Armenia's major industries. Cash-strapped Armenia had no alternative but to hand over the shares, which it did in a 2002 treaty candidly titled "Possessions in Exchange for Debt"—a reminder of the infamous debt-for-equity swaps of the Yeltsin years (another Chubais invention), which spawned Russia's oligarchs.

Russia's second step in rebuilding its empire in the Caucasus is to unite itself and Armenia in a single economic zone. Because Georgia stands directly in the geographical path to realizing this goal, Russia had to deal with it first. In the 1990s, it used crude political pressure to bring Georgia in line, but it shifted to economic leverage in 2003. When US-based AES Silk Road failed to transform Georgia's energy system, Chubais's RAO UES bought AES's holdings and other assets that amounted to 75 percent of the country's electricity network.

Then came Georgia's Rose Revolution. Many state-owned firms were privatized for ten times the sums yielded in asset sales under the previous government of Eduard Shevardnadze.

But an utter lack of transparency allowed Russian companies—and their subsidiaries registered in third countries—to snap up most of the new offerings. Typical was the Russian holding company Promyslennye investory (Industrial Investors), which managed to get a major gold mine and then half of a plant producing gold alloys.

Russia's main foreign policy instrument in Georgia is Gazprom, the state-controlled gas monopoly. Gazprom's aim is to control not only the gas industry in Georgia but also the only pipeline that feeds Russian gas to both Georgia and Armenia. Had the United States not intervened in 2005 with $49.5 million to rehabilitate the pipeline, it would have ended up in Gazprom's hands. Even then, pressure from Moscow may result in joint Russian-Georgian control of the pipeline, if not its outright sale to Gazprom. The Georgian government, without clear support from the West, may yet agree to such a deal, something that Moldova, which saw its gas cut off on January 1, has just done.

Gazprom is not the only state entity carrying out Russian policy in the South Caucasus. In 2004, Russia's state-owned Vneshtorgbank acquired a controlling stake in Armenia's Armsberbank. The following year, Vneshtorgbank purchased a controlling stake in the privatized United Georgian Bank, Georgia's third largest. In effect, Vneshtorgbank renationalized United Georgian Bank, but the new owner was the Russian state.

Recently, Chubais's RAO UES has had the lead role in integrating Georgia into Russia's liberal empire. When the Georgian authorities announced plans to privatize the Inguri Power Plant and renew construction of the long-stalled Khudoni Power Plant, slated to become Georgia's largest, RAO UES immediately began staking out a dominant role for itself in both projects. The combination of massive pressure from the Russian side and silence from the West could leave Georgia's entire power system, both gas and electricity, in Russian hands.

Russia's scheme to rehabilitate the rail line from its territory into the secessionist Georgian province of Abkhazia similarly mixes economics with neo-imperial aspirations. Even though it is focused on land that the United Nations recognizes as part of Georgia, the main beneficiaries of this project would be Russia and Armenia.

If the international community allows this scheme to go forward, it will have endorsed Russia's effort to separate Abkhazia from Georgia. Parallel with this, Russia and Armenia are planning a new rail link to Iran. Besides its obvious benefits to Iranian President Mahmoud Ahmadinejad's retrograde government, this will deftly weaken the South Caucasus's links with the West, which the United States and Europe have spent a decade fostering.

Russia's effort to entrap Georgia and its neighbors in the nets of its new liberal empire is part of a well-coordinated attempt to reorient the South Caucasus as a whole toward the anti-Western coalition of Russia and Iran. Western countries, and the United States in particular, must provide firm backing and support to the South Caucasus to prevent Russia from realizing its destabilizing and dangerous neo-imperial dream.

Russia's Illiberal "Liberal Empire"

February 28, 2006[*]

Across the West, many people are questioning whether Russia will continue using natural gas as a means of putting economic and political pressure on Ukraine, Georgia, and other countries in what the Kremlin regards as its "near abroad." Using the energy weapon, however, is not just a tactic: it is at the heart of the prevailing doctrine guiding Russian foreign policy.

Russia's policy toward the post-Soviet countries is based on the doctrine of a "liberal empire," according to which Russia's major government-owned and private companies should assume control of key economic entities across the territories of the former Soviet republics by acquiring their assets. In this context, the word *liberal* should be understood to

---

[*] V. Papava, "Russia's Illiberal 'Liberal Empire,'" *Project Syndicate*, February 28, 2006, https://www.project-syndicate.org/commentary/russia-s-illiberal--liberal-empire.

suggest that the empire of the "new Russian dream" should be built by purely economic means, excluding all forcible action against other nations.

Naturally, the key role in this model is given to the supply of energy to the post-Soviet countries. In particular, the Russian utility giant Gazprom uses increases in gas prices as a means to punish "disobedient" neighbors. Ukraine was punished in this way for its eagerness to integrate with the West following the Orange Revolution. However, after the return of the pro-Russian Victor Yanukovych to the position of Ukrainian prime minister, the country's pro-Western orientation has been significantly weakened. So it should be no surprise that Ukraine under Yanukovych has faced no further problems with the supply of Russian gas.

But Georgia remains a major Kremlin-Gazprom target. Russia's attempt to drag Georgia into its imperial net started in the summer of 2003, when the Russian power monopoly United Energy System took control of 75 percent of Georgia's electricity network. After the Rose Revolution of November 2003, Russian companies turned out to be the most avid purchasers of Georgian enterprises and their assets.

The first significant obstacle in the way of Russia's designs on Georgia was intervention by the United States, which demanded that the Georgian government drop negotiations with Gazprom and banned Georgia from selling the gas pipeline that connects Russia and Armenia through Georgian territory. Russia punished Georgia almost immediately, banning the import of Georgian wines and mineral waters—both key export goods.

As Georgia's prospects of joining NATO seemed to increase, Russian actions became more illiberal. Ethnic Georgians living in Russia, including those who were Russian citizens, became targets of persecution. Russia's actions were aimed at fomenting an anti-government backlash in Georgia, thereby paving the way for pro-Russian political forces to come to power.

But the illiberalism inherent in Russian imperialism is not limited to recent behavior, and, more disturbingly, it extends to the question of Georgia's territorial integrity, as Russian troops continue to prop up secessionist regions. By provoking ethnic conflicts in the territories of former Soviet republics, Moscow hopes to keep them under its control and influence. Ironically, the Russian troops deployed in the renegade Georgian regions of Abkhazia and South Ossetia have been accorded the status of peacekeepers. But they are really illegal occupiers, as Russia's decision to give Russian passports to these regions' residents attests.

Now Russia is threatening to recognize the independence of Abkhazia and South Ossetia if the West recognizes the Serbian province of Kosovo as an independent nation. To the extent that most of the residents of Abkhazia and South Ossetia have already been given Russian citizenship, the recognition of those two regions' sovereignty would be entirely fictitious and, in fact, an interim measure on the way to their full annexation by Russia.

To strengthen Russia's political influence over Georgia's separatist regions, Gazprom, without taking the trouble to ask for permission from Georgia's democratically elected leaders, has begun constructing a gas pipeline connecting Russia and South Ossetia directly. Although there was no interruption of gas supply from Tbilisi to South Ossetia, this step is necessary for the Kremlin to ensure even greater integration of this Georgian region into Russia's economic system.

With Gazprom having already doubled gas tariffs for Georgia, the energy noose is tightening. But, thanks to gas supplies from neighboring Azerbaijan, Georgia has not yet been strangled.

A revived Russian empire, whether it is constructed by force or through economic coercion, is not in anyone's interests. Reigning in Russia's illiberal liberal empire is the central question of European security today.

Georgia's Hollow Revolution

February 27, 2008[*]

Introduction

On November 7, 2007—ninety years to the day after the Bolsheviks successfully set in motion events that would culminate in the communists taking power in Russia—the world again witnessed a political uprising with the potential to reshape a nation, this time in Russia's southern neighbor, the Republic of Georgia. But whereas the 1917 Bolshevik coup d'état ultimately succeeded, the consequences of last year's events in the Georgian capital, Tbilisi, remain less than certain.

Four years after hailing the Rose Revolution as putting the former Soviet satellite on the road toward capitalism and

---

[*] V. Papava, "Georgia's Hollow Revolution: Does Georgia's Pro-Western and Anti-Russian Policy Amount to Democracy?" *The Harvard International Review*, February 27, 2008, http://hir.harvard.edu/article/?a=1682.

democracy, observers in the West were stunned by the events of November 2007: the suppression of a peaceful demonstration, the shutdown of opposition TV channels, and the declaration of a state of emergency. However, for those analysts following events from within the country, it was hardly a surprise.

Still, much was left to consider. Why were the events of November 2007 unforeseen by the international community, and in particular, the West? And why, until November 2007, did Georgia's postrevolution leadership remain so attractive to observers in the West, even while analysts within the country grew increasingly disillusioned?

In this article, I seek to answer these questions by taking a closer look at developments in Georgia since the Rose Revolution. By doing so, I seek to demonstrate why the events of November 2007 were inevitable and how they stemmed from the Georgian government's departure from the democratic ideals of the Rose Revolution.

Postrevolution Challenges and the President's Centralization of Power

Georgia's new, mostly young, and in many respects inexperienced government inherited many problems from the prior Shevardnadze administration. An ongoing energy crisis meant yet another winter with electricity and heating shortages. An inability or unwillingness to collect taxes had left pensions and government salaries unpaid, and rampant corruption rendered the government inefficient and ineffective.

Citing the need to address these challenges, as well as the need to restore the country's territorial integrity (two separatist regions, Abkhazia and South Ossetia, had declared independence in the early 1990s and a third region, Ajara, while nominally loyal to Tbilisi, remained under de facto control of a local strongman), the postrevolution government of President Mikheil Saakashvili set about concentrating power in the executive from almost the moment it took power.

In February 2004, just a few weeks after the election, constitutional amendments were rushed through parliament granting the president the power to dismiss the government and, in the event of deadlock, to disband the parliament altogether and order new parliamentary elections. The natural consequence was a parliamentary body loyal not only to the president but also to his government. This significantly weakened its independence and ability to check executive authority.

Although in late 2006, under pressure from the Council of Europe, Saakashvili proposed a further amendment to the constitution that would allow for an extraordinary presidential election in case of repeated dismissals of the parliament, it was largely a token reform. Despite this minor adjustment to the balance of power, other changes in the election schedule further strengthened presidential influence over the parliament. Previously, new parliamentary and presidential elections were due for spring 2008 and winter 2009, respectively, but the amendments rescheduled both to autumn 2008. Thus, although the president reduced his term by a few months, he extended the parliament's term by more than half a year—an astute move guaranteed to bolster the president's party, which, though the majority, was losing public support every day.

Additionally, prior to the events of November 7, 2007, Saakashvili had no significant competitors in the future presidential race. Hence, the change substantially increased the likelihood that those who would vote for Saakashvili would also vote for his party for parliament in future elections.

Thus, even before the crackdown of November 7, 2007, the key plan of Saakashvili and his allies was greater concentration of executive power by maintaining parliamentary loyalty. Although some parliamentary opposition remained, it served more as a decoration, ironically necessary for the democratic image of the Rose Revolution that Saakashvili's administration sought to maintain.

A Stronger Executive and a Stronger State

This concentration of power did little to advance democracy, but it was not entirely without benefit. For one thing, stronger presidential powers allowed Saakashvili's government to restore financial order and increase tax revenues, overcoming the budgetary crisis inherited from the Shevardnadze era and allowing Georgia to pay off all accumulated debts to pensioners and public sector employees. Additionally, after the revolution in 2004 in the Autonomous Republic of Ajara, new opportunities emerged for arranging a normal budgeting process between the central government and the formerly separatist region.

As a result of the changes that took place in Ajara, tax revenues of the national budget during 2004 significantly increased for the first time since Georgia's independence in 1991. In the summer of 2004, the International Monetary Fund (IMF) renewed its funding program, which had been terminated in 2003 due to the incompetence and corruption of the Shevardnadze administration, further illustrating the country's financial turnaround.

The new government also fought crime and corruption. Stronger presidential powers enabled it to abolish the much-detested traffic police and to quickly create a Western-style police patrol. Targeting corruption in the energy sector also paid dividends, yielding a much more reliable supply of electricity. Additionally, to further reduce endemic corruption, the government introduced national examinations for admission to universities, abolishing the Soviet-era legacy of separate corruption-prone admission exams to individual universities.

Former government officials and their relatives guilty of corrupt practices were arrested and only released upon paying the "price of liberty." This created an additional revenue stream for the government, which was then paid into extra-budgetary law-enforcement development accounts. The practice was promoted as returning stolen state money and property, as well as creating an additional source of revenue. However, this practice was not a sustainable source of revenue.

Broad and ambitious economic reforms, such as large-scale privatization, simplified business-licensing practices, and the reduction of tax and tariff rates also accompanied the expansion of executive authority and garnered much international attention. In addition, Georgia's improved financial situation allowed the postrevolution government to radically overhaul the Armed Forces of Georgia. With additional assistance from the United States and other NATO member states, military readiness has improved greatly, and Georgian forces serving in Iraq and Afghanistan have received high marks from coalition officials.

Setbacks for Democracy

But much of this progress has come at a cost. For starters, the subordination of the legislature to the executive lessened any sense of government officials' accountability. This has produced many instances of gross disrespect for the rule of law. The parliament has become so weakened that it is now called the "government's notary."

In addition to the weakening of parliament, the judiciary has lost its strength and independence. Today, it is run by the general prosecutor's office, firmly rooting it within the executive branch.

The postrevolution government has also claimed greater control over the media, especially television. Many independent TV stations and popular newspapers were closed shortly after the Rose Revolution. While several private stations were permitted to continue operating, they are now effectively under state control. This has resulted in the freedom of press being severely curtailed—a major setback for democratic development, but a setback largely unnoticed by Saakashvili's Western friends.

Sweeping staffing and institutional reforms were often poorly considered. Most experienced civil servants were dismissed (often illegally) and replaced by younger and frequently foreign-educated staffers, resulting in a significant loss of institutional memory. These problems were further compounded when nonprofessional cabinet ministers were named and assignment of responsibility became arbitrary.

A notable example of these practices came in late 2004, when the state antimonopoly service was abolished. In 2007, its functions were reassigned to the Ministry of the Interior, thus making the ministry responsible not only for crime and police but also business. Another notable example came in spring 2006, when the task of marketing Georgian wines abroad was delegated to the Minister of Defense.

The revolutionary wave emboldened the government to reorganize a number of ministries and departments. In particular, the State Department of Statistics, which before the revolution had been an independent agency accountable to the president, was folded into the Ministry of Economic Development, despite the inherent conflict of interest between the two entities. As a result, statistics in Georgia now play the same role as they did in the Soviet Union: a political function to proclaim annual improvement in the country's economy.

For example, in an "accidental leak" in August 2006, the department declared that the annual inflation rate in Georgia had reached 14.5 percent in July. After receiving strong criticism from the IMF, the government dismissed the head of the department and charged his successor with reducing inflation. By December 2006, the government was reporting an inflation rate of 9.2 percent. Nominally satisfied, the IMF was content to turn a blind eye.

Disrespect for Property Rights

While the postrevolution government has been widely hailed for fighting corruption, in practice, corruption in Georgia has been transformed, not eliminated. Spending from extrabudgetary accounts, at the discretion of the executive, has not been subject to public scrutiny. The problem has only become more acute since the government started to replenish those accounts with "voluntary contributions" from businesses. Further, if prerevolution functionaries had pockets open for bribes, their successors, though they may have had closed pockets, certainly had open bank accounts.

These accounts were initially ignored by the IMF, which largely regarded them as a lesser of two evils. However, the IMF was ultimately forced to recognize that the use of these accounts was a futile attempt to beat corruption while allowing corruption. It was not until spring 2006, under IMF pressure, that the extrabudgetary accounts being used for illicit donations were finally abolished.

Becoming European

Ultimately, the government's disrespect for the constitution and the rule of law was made most evident with respect to property rights. In instances of privatization of state-owned property, new owners seemingly emerged from nowhere. Deprivatization—that is, the taking back of property that had been privatized before the revolution—had also been prone to injustice: property has often been reclaimed forcibly by the government through its law-enforcement entities, the general prosecutor's office and the Ministry of the Interior.

Based on the recipients of this reclaimed property, it would appear that the real goal of deprivatization has been the redistribution of property for the benefit of the newly formed elite, not for the benefit of the public. And although thus far deprivatization has only been widely pursued once, there is no guarantee that another round is not in the offing.

The government's rejection of property rights has extended to extralegal decisions to demolish privately owned houses built before the revolution, even when owners have documentation of ownership and legitimacy of construction. In many instances, the government's only stated argument was a desire to improve the city's image. However, these practices have largely evaded Western attention. In fact, in the World Bank's *Doing Business 2007* report, Georgia was ranked as the world's eighteenth best place for businesses, despite the number of instances of impropriety by the government with respect to private property.

Vladimer Papava

Continued Corruption Among Elites

While the campaign against petty corruption has largely been successful, corruption among elites continues to be a problem for the government. This came to the surface most notably when Irakli Okruashvili, the former defense minister and onetime member of the president's inner circle, was charged with corruption—but only *after* forming an opposition party and making scandalous accusations against Saakashvili. In addition to revealing that corruption continues among the postrevolution elite, the episode put other officials on notice that their corrupt behaviors will be exposed should they dare to join the opposition. As a result, while the government's campaign against corruption has largely been a success for the state in terms of efficiency, it has also been an opportunity for the Saakashvili administration to silence dissent. The campaign has actually been a setback for the cause of real democracy.

Even more troubling are the reports of human rights abuses by the government. These reports, which include alleged murders by the police and have been detailed in numerous reports by public defenders, have both troubled the public and contributed to a sense among Georgians that the police are not being adequately punished for abuse. Still, these instances of police brutality and human rights abuses have generally provoked little criticism from the West. As a result, the Saakashvili government has had little incentive to exercise restraint.

Why Has the West Turned a Blind Eye?

While the Saakashvili government's achievements were enthusiastically received in the West, its failures were typically subject to moderate criticism at best. So why did it take the extreme events of November 7 to finally prompt serious criticism in the West of Mikheil Saakashvili, along with his government and the parliamentary majority? And why has the West not held the postrevolution government of Georgia to a higher standard?

For one thing, the West was captivated by Saakashvili. A post-Soviet leader with a Western university education, Saakasvili in his rhetoric has been a passionate advocate of democratic values, human rights, and a market economy. Official statements regarding Georgia's desire to join NATO and the EU, and its participation in the coalition in Iraq and peacekeeping operations in Kosovo and Afghanistan, were regarded as further proof of the postrevolution government's Western orientation (even though these policies were also in place under Shevardnadze) and further galvanized his support in foreign capitals.

But in contrast to his engaging manner with Western audiences, his rhetoric in Georgia had a much blunter edge. In one appearance on Georgian TV, for example, he said that the senior generation of Georgian scholars and public figures must be "flushed down." This hostility, and his numerous policy failings, led many within Georgia to see Saakashvili as an authoritarian ruler and to see Georgia's embryonic democracy as growing weaker by the day.

The West also liked Saakashvili's consistently anti-Russian rhetoric and typically tough (and sometimes cynical) criticism of Russia's political leadership. But very little attention was paid to the fact that, after the Rose Revolution, Georgia opened its doors to Russian capital, which has continued to flow despite the embargo on Georgian exports that Russia initiated in spring 2006. The Kremlin's open and intense dislike for Georgia's postrevolution government and Saakashvili in particular—manifested in bombardments of Georgian territory and de facto annexation of Abkhazia and South Ossetia by issuing Russian passports to their inhabitants—only reinforced the West's longstanding support for Georgia and its leadership.

In short, Georgia's pro-Western and anti-Russian course compelled the West to turn a blind eye to the postrevolution government's failings and excesses—a fact that did not go unnoticed by the Saakashvili administration. After US President George W. Bush visited Georgia in May 2005, the Georgian leadership behaved as if the visit by itself exonerated it for antidemocratic actions past and future.

Lessons of the Rose Revolution

In the end, what Georgia's experience calls to light is the folly of equating a pro-Western and anti-Russian orientation with democracy. For Georgians, the lesson is often expressed with dark humor and biting cynicism: "Don't upset me while I'm building democracy, or I'll kill you all!"

The experience of Georgia also calls to light the West's double standard for democracy: one for itself and another for countries like Georgia. Although postrevolution Georgia had been hailed as a rising democracy, in reality, Georgia's government has resembled authoritarianism more than democracy. But by not taking a stronger stand toward the Saakashvili government on the disparity between its lofty rhetoric and actual governance, the West is ultimately undermining its own ideals, since Georgians are beginning to equate a pro-Western government with a more authoritarian one.

Epilogue

Following the dramatic public backlash against his government's failures and shortly after the events of November 7, 2007, Saakashvili resigned and called for a new presidential election on January 5, 2008 to rescue his own image and Georgia's image. (The Georgian constitution requires that a sitting president resign at least forty-five days before standing for reelection.) Similarly, parliamentary elections were tentatively moved up to spring 2008.

Still, despite this token democratic gesture to appease the public, during the presidential campaign it was apparent that Saakashvili, though technically no longer in office, was still using administrative resources for his own interests, directing government officials, and appearing at public openings of civil projects.

Considering the circumstances, the elections were competitive, and polling was mostly uneventful. In the final accounting, Saakashvili received more than half the total vote, thus averting a runoff. Although international observers gave qualified approval to the campaign environment and elections conduct, Georgian watchdog groups have expressed serious reservations about the transparency and fairness of the ballot counting, and the opposition continues to protest the results.

Given the progress and setbacks since the Rose Revolution four years ago, and the gravity of the events of November 2007, this postelection period will be critical. Georgia faces the real possibility of further sliding toward the Russian model of so-called managed or sovereign democracy, which is really just authoritarianism in disguise. The West's active engagement will be critical to avoiding this outcome, and for this reason, with elections now complete and the lessons from November 2007 made painfully clear, Georgians can only hope that the West will no longer blindly trust Georgia's newly elected president and parliament, and instead hold both to a higher standard.

Pipeline Harmonization Instead of Alternative Pipelines: Why the Pipeline "Cold War" Needs to End

with Mikheil Tokmazishvili

June 15, 2008[*]

The countries of the European Union (EU) are now so dependent on Russian energy resources that this has given Moscow a highly effective tool to put political pressure not only on them but also on countries like Belarus and Ukraine

---

[*] V. Papava and M. Tokmazishvili, "Pipeline Harmonization Instead of Alternative Pipelines: Why the Pipeline 'Cold War' Needs to End," *Azerbaijan in the World: The Electronic Publication of Azerbaijan Diplomatic Academy* 1, no. 10, June 15, 2008, http://biweekly.ada.edu.az/vol_1_no_10/Pipeline_harmonization_instead_of_alternative_pipelines.htm.

across which these resources flow to reach Europe. Not surprisingly, EU countries have looked for other sources, including the Caspian Basin states. But what is troubling is that these sources are inevitably modified by adjectives like *alternative*, a conscious or unconscious reflection of a view that there is an inherent confrontation between Russia and the rest of the world on energy issues.

Some commentators now speak of a "pipeline confrontation" or even of a "pipeline cold war," terms that have been linked to pipelines like Baku-Tbilisi-Supsa (BTS), Baku-Tbilisi-Ceyhan (BTC), and the South Caucasus Pipeline (SCP). But such commentators forget that these pipelines carry less than 10 percent of the amount of oil that Russian pipelines do and less than 5 percent of the gas, figures that call into question their utility as alternatives to Russian pipelines.

Moscow is at least in part to blame for this situation. It has used its monopolistic position in this sector to promote a wide range of interests. Moreover, it has opposed the construction of alternatives lest its own position be somehow weakened. More than a decade ago, the Russian government opposed the BTC project, despite instability in the North Caucasus through which its own pipeline passed. And when common sense prevailed and the BTC project advanced, Moscow never acknowledged its error and continues to try to block the completion of other pipeline systems.

Now, given the world's thirst for hydrocarbons, the time has come to shift from the alternative pipelines paradigm to a new one of mutually supplementary pipelines or even pipeline harmonization. If that perspective is adopted, then analysts and governments can view the pipelines as a single whole with a single purpose: providing an uninterrupted and consistent supply of energy resources to their customers.

In terms of this paradigm, transportation of Caspian energy resources to the West should be viewed not as competitors to Russian routes but as supplements to them. Indeed, several important steps have been taken in this direction. In January 2007, Kazakhstan and those developing the Kashagan and Tengiz oil fields signed an Memorandum of Understanding on the construction of a Kazakhstan-Caspian Transportation System intended to ensure the outflow of growing amounts of oil through the Caspian region. Oil is to be moved along the Eskene-Kurik-Baku-Tbilisi-Ceyhan route, something that will require the building of the Eskene-Kurik oil pipeline. And in March 2007, Russia, Bulgaria and Greece signed an intergovernmental agreement to build the Trans-Balkan Oil Pipeline, Burgas-Alexandropolis, which would begin in the Bulgarian Black Sea port of Burgas and end at Alexandroupolis on the Greek Aegean coast.

Harmonizing gas pipelines is even more important given that it is far from clear that the Russian gas transport system will be sufficient to transport expanded volumes of Central Asian gas during the first part of the next decade. As far as the Trans-Caspian pipeline is concerned, it is far from clear just who will be involved and how various interests will be harmonized. It is associated in the minds of most with the Nabucco and the White Stream gas projects, a structure that will both complete and complement the South Stream gas pipeline Moscow hopes to run to Varna in Bulgaria and then further west.

If all the countries of the region and their customers recognize just how large the demand from the latter is likely to be, they should be able to cooperate rather than compete in the construction of pipelines and thus provide the best possible supplies of oil and gas to the Europeans.

5

Central Caucaso-Asia: Toward a Redefinition of Post-Soviet Central Eurasia

October 1, 2008[*]

The disintegration of the Soviet Union not only resulted in the rise of a group of new independent states but their integration into newly defined geopolitical areas. In recent years, the term *Central Eurasia*, which refers to Azerbaijan, Armenia, Georgia, Kazakhstan, Kyrgyzstan, Tajikistan, Turkmenistan, and Uzbekistan, has been attracting attention as a distinct geopolitical area.

---

[*] V. Papava, "Central Caucaso-Asia: Toward a Redefinition of Post-Soviet Central Eurasia," *Azerbaijan in the World: The Electronic Publication of Azerbaijan Diplomatic Academy* I, no. 17, October 1, 2008, http://biweekly.ada.edu.az/vol_1_no_17/Toward_a_redefinition_of_post-Soviet_Central_Eurasia.htm.

Vladimer Papava

There are at least two ways to think about the Eurasian continent in geopolitical terms. The first focuses on the European and Asian geographic dimensions in its geopolitical vision of the continent (e.g. Brzezinski 1997). The other approach, which arises from a Eurasianist conception of the region drawing mainly on geography (Bassin 1991, 14), equates Russia with Eurasia (Lewis and Wigen 1997, 222; also Hauner 1994, 217), an idea that has become popular and much debated in the post-Soviet period (Hauner 1994, 222). The Russian geopolitical school's vision of Eurasia thus embodies Russia's old imperial ambitions, and consequently, those who speak about Central Eurasia in terms of Azerbaijan, Armenia, Georgia, Kazakhstan, Kyrgyzstan, Tajikistan, Turkmenistan, and Uzbekistan—leaving aside such territories like Afghanistan, Northern Iran, the Northern Caucasus, Northwestern China, Cashmere, and the Tibetan Plateau—are reflecting a Russian understanding that others have disputed (Weisbrode 2001, 11–12).

Some geopolitical studies still follow the Soviet tradition and define Central Asia as including only five former Soviet republics—Kazakhstan, Kyrgyzstan, Tajikistan, Turkmenistan, and Uzbekistan—a definition that leaves out Afghanistan, Mongolia, and adjacent areas (Naby 1994, 35–36). Another term, *Greater Central Asia*, is sometimes applied to the five former Soviet republics plus Afghanistan (Starr 2005).

The Caucasus as a geopolitical term appeared when Russia conquered the region. It was divided between the

Becoming European

Trans-Caucasus, the area south of the main Caucasus ridge, and the North Caucasus, the area to the north of the ridge. The North Caucasus is now part of the Russian Federation, whereas the Trans-Caucasus is the portion south of it to the edge of Russian imperial expansion. After the USSR disappeared, the term *Trans-Caucasus* was replaced with the more correct *South Caucasus*, with Russian writers alone using the former.

Viewed from a non-Russian perspective, *the Caucasus* includes not only Armenia, Azerbaijan, Georgia, and the Russian North Caucasus but also northeastern Turkish areas—the *ils* of Agri, Ardahan, Artvin, Van, Igdyr, and Kars—and the northwestern parts of Iran—the *ostanha* of eastern Azerbaijan—Ardabil, Gilyan, Zanjan, Qazvin, Hamadan, and Western Azerbaijan (Ismailov and Kengerli 2003). That division reflects the reality that all these regions have been populated by Caucasian peoples from time immemorial.

From this, it follows that the Caucasus region consists not of two parts, as the Russians insist, but of three: the Central Caucasus, made up of the three independent states of Azerbaijan, Armenia, and Georgia; the Northern Caucasus, consisting of Russia's autonomous units bordering on the Caucasus; the Southern Caucasus, which covers the *ils* of Turkey bordering on Azerbaijan, Armenia, and Georgia—the Southwestern Caucasus; and the northwestern *ostanha* of Iran—the Southeastern Caucasus (Ismailov and Kengerli 2003).

If we proceed from the fact that the eight countries discussed here form two subregions—the Central Caucasus and Central Asia—the larger region, which includes both subregions, should be called the Central Caucaso-Asia (in Russian, Kavkazia), as this preserves the term *Central* as the key one for both regions, while the new term *Caucaso-Asia* or *Caucasasia* (Papava 2008).

The newly coined term *Central Caucaso-Asia* reflects a conceptual idea of the interests of strengthening the local countries' state sovereignty, which, in principle, contradicts the spirit and idea of Russo-centric Eurasianism. And this implicit pro-Western vector better suits the interests of these countries for stronger sovereignty, greater democratization, and the expansion of a market economy.

References

Bassin, M. 1991. "Russia Between Europe and Asia: The Ideological Construction of Geopolitical Space." *Slavic Review* 50 (1): 1–17.

Brzezinski, Z. 1997. *The Grand Chessboard. American Primacy and Its Geostrategic Imperatives.* New York: Basic Books.

Hauner, M. L. 1994. "The Disintegration of the Soviet Eurasian Empire: An Ongoing Debate." In *Central Asia and the Caucasus After the Soviet Union*, edited by M. Mesbahi, 209–223. Gainesville: University Press of Florida.

Ismailov, E., and Z. Kengerli. 2003. "The Caucasus in the Globalizing World: A New Integration Model." *Central Asia and the Caucasus*, no. 2: 135–44.

Lewis, M. W., and K. E. Wigen. 1997. *The Myth of Continents: A Critique of Metageography.* Berkley: University of California Press.

Naby, E. 1994. "The Emerging Central Asia: Ethnic and Religious Factions." In *Central Asia and the Caucasus After the Soviet Union*, edited by M. Mesbahi, 34–55. Gainesville: University Press of Florida.

Papava, V. 2008. "'Central Caucasasia' Instead of 'Central Eurasia.'" *Central Asia and the Caucasus* no. 2: 30–42.

Starr, F. S. 2005. *A 'Greater Central Asia Partnership' for Afghanistan and Its Neighbors*. Silk Road Paper, March. Washington, DC: Central Asia-Caucasus Institute, Johns Hopkins University-SAIS, http://www.stimson.org/newcentury/pdf/Strategy.pdf (last accessed September 19, 2008).

Weisbrode, K. 2001. *Central Eurasia: Prize or Quicksand? Contenting Views of Instability in Karabakh, Ferghana, and Afghanistan*. New York: Oxford University Press.

6

Russia: Being in the Kremlin Means Never Letting Go

November 5, 2008[*]

In the years immediately following the Soviet collapse of 1991, Russia was so weak that it found itself dependent on Western support, and therefore it felt obligated to accept Western values. Some in the West were lulled into a false sense of security, but the reality is that many Russians never really let go of their old way of thinking and their nostalgia for empire.

This nostalgia was a chief motivation for Russia's incursion into Georgia in August and its high-handed actions since then. (For background, see the *Eurasia Insight* archive.) What we are seeing now is a Kremlin that seeks to avenge the humiliation that Russia suffered throughout the Gorbachev and Yeltsin

---

[*] V. Papava, "Russia: Being in the Kremlin Means Never Letting Go," *Eurasia Insight, Eurasianet*, November 5, 2008, https://eurasianet.org/russia-being-in-the-kremlin-means-never-letting-go.

Becoming European

eras. Profound shifts in the global energy landscape have made possible Russia's quest to restore at least some semblance of the old, shattered empire. As Europe currently receives roughly 40 percent of its natural gas from Russia, it is Brussels that now must be careful not to offend Moscow.

The United States, with its ill-fated rush into Iraq, also had a hand in enabling the return of aggressive nationalism in Russia. The Kremlin thinking went like this: If the United States could initiate a "preemptive" war against Iraq, why couldn't Russia do the same, and in a neighboring country, no less? Russian policymakers, as has been widely publicized, saw no difference in the US recognition of Kosovo's independence and Russia's desire to change the status of the separatist entities of Abkhazia and South Ossetia.

Finally, Georgia's aspirations to gain membership in NATO struck a raw nerve in the Kremlin, reviving memories of past insults to Russia's dignity as a great power. Filtered through the prism of Moscow's twisted logic, the West pushed Russia into making the move into Georgia.

It's not such a surprise that Georgia became Russia's first target. Georgia proper, as well as Abkhazia and South Ossetia, border on Russia. For years, the West was reluctant to acknowledge that Tbilisi's key problem in Abkhazia and South Ossetia had its origins in Moscow—namely the Kremlin's decision to grant Russian citizenship to residents of the two regions.

Euphoric from the success of its military action in Georgia, the Kremlin precipitously recognized the independence of both breakaway regions. In doing so, Moscow now finds itself caught in a paradox: it acknowledged the independence of two entities in which the majority of residents hold Russian citizenship. While the Kremlin is fond of drawing parallels between the Abkhazia/South Ossetia and Kosovo, it must be remembered that before recognizing Kosovo's independence, neither the United States nor any other country encouraged people there to accept American or any other citizenship.

We can expect that, after a respectful pause, the Kremlin will instruct the puppet governments of Abkhazia and South Ossetia to hold referenda concerning the territories' incorporation into the Russian Federation. The outcomes of such referenda, of course, will be a foregone conclusion. We can also expect that Moscow will offer convoluted justifications for annexation. For example, one argument might say that if the global community, outside of Russia and a few maverick states, continues to withhold recognition of Abkhazia and South Ossetia, then the peoples of those states will have little option other than joining Russia.

By this, the Kremlin stands to accomplish the treacherous objectives it has been pursuing for years. The most galling aspect of Russia's nefarious plan is that Moscow will try to avoid taking responsibility for its actions. Instead, it will pin the blame on the West, which, through its reluctance to recognize Abkhazia and South Ossetia, will be "forcing" Russia to absorb the two territories into the federation.

Georgia's "Green Friday"

November 17, 2008[*]

When talking about the strengthening of the American dollar in Georgia, we must take two factors into account. Firstly, this is not necessarily a Georgian trend but a global one. This is an American response to the global financial crisis and the outcome of a historic decision by the US administration to inject USD 700 billion to support financial markets. This has resulted in gradual appreciation of the American currency and the current global trend. Secondly, the sharp drop of the Georgian lari against the dollar is credited to factors of Georgian origin.

While the world is tackling the global financial meltdown, Georgia has seen a dramatic slump in foreign investments.

---

[*] V. Papava, "Georgia's 'Green Friday,'" *The Georgian Times*, November 17, 2008, http://geotimes.ge/_old/archive/index.php?m=home&newsid=13663.

The five-day war in August has further scared off investors. They are still worried about the stability of the investment environment and fear that a Russian invasion may occur again. This has led to the fall of foreign currency inflows into Georgia.

The global financial crisis has also affected the remittances that Georgians living abroad send to their families back home as their earnings shrank. This has further weighed down the GEL.

Under these circumstances, Georgia has two options. The first is that the national currency will start a gradual, creeping devaluation that allows banks, businesses, and people to adapt to the changes as they witness the downturn and it becomes more predictable. There are no drastic changes, and everyone proceeds with their financial operations. The second is the sharp fall of the GEL when the central bank decides to turn the currency from one rate to another abruptly.

The creeping devaluation of the lari engenders Georgian exports, as local entrepreneurs prefer foreign currency and view exports as the best way to get it. Given that imports outnumber exports in Georgia by a factor of four, the slow devaluation of the lari is a very good scheme for promoting exports.

The creeping devaluation itself has two scenarios: one is when the downturn is very slow and is difficult to even notice, and the second is when the lari slides 0.5 tetri a day on average. In Georgia's case, it would be certainly better if the lari decreased 0.5 tetri per day, which would allow businesses

Becoming European

and people to adapt. The Georgian central bank, the National Bank of Georgia (NBG), would have to spend fewer reserves.

However, the policy the NBG has been pursuing was based on creating illusory stability. The lari was falling 0.1 tetri average, which suggested nothing. There was an illusion that nothing was happening. In reality, if we look at the data posted on the NBG website, we will see that this cost NBG dearly. The average demand was USD 10–25 million per day, and the NBG had to sell reserves to meet the demand. As a consequence, it sold USD 30 million from its reserves in a month, which resulted in depreciation of the GEL only for 3.5 tetri.

Interesting as it is, after the August war, the IMF earmarked USD 750 million for a standby arrangement, and the money went to the NBG reserves to maintain the lari's stability. USD 250 million has been already provided, and it has been already spent.

The second option is a sharp fall of the lari as the NBG abruptly decides to turn the currency from one rate to another. This would cause shock and panic unless the government followed up with a timely explanation. When the currency slumps, the feeling of stability disappears. Everyone tries to get rid of lari from their pockets or deposit and convert lari into dollars or euros. This causes a snowball effect, increasing the demand on foreign currency and further drowning the lari—an artificial stimulation of sharp devaluation. As a consequence of the dollarization of economic growth, banks refuse to issue credits in lari, as trust of the government and the NBG declines. Such a fall is destructive for the banking sector and for the monetary system as a whole.

Some 80 percent of Georgian consumer products are imported, and the price of the imported goods is certainly tied to foreign currency. When the downturn is slow, importers are able to adapt to it. But when the GEL slumps, say, 21 points (depreciation by 15 percent) and importers take losses, they have to think about getting it back by setting a higher margin. The price would also reflect the expectations that importers have after seeing slumps in the exchange rate.

It should be taken into account that, after the American dollar gained heavily, the NBG withdrew lari surpluses from the market. This seems to be a good thing, as reducing the money supply in general curbs inflation. But to cut inflation, you need not just withdraw the money supply but also focus on where the remaining money will go. During the crisis, consumers have to redistribute their resources to primary needs, which cost more. In the end, this leads to a decline in the standard of living.

What benefits does the government receive from the sharp fall in the national currency? At a glance, it generates additional revenues from imports initially, as the price of imported commodities is tied to the foreign currency—the American dollar or euro. This is an ad valorem tax that is paid to the budget in lari. Additional revenues in GEL will be generated from international donor support. As the American dollar rises, more tax revenues flow into the budget, and the government seems to have profited.

But the government in reality is losing. In economic theory, this is known as the Oliver-Tanzi Effect. Although more money comes in, the purchasing power of the currency is low, and government expenditure is less effective. So the government loses.

Trading at the Interbank Currency Exchange (ICE) started as usual on Friday, November 7. The demand by commercial banks was USD 31 million. Once the first operation at USD 270,000 was over, the ICE suddenly stopped trading, citing technical reasons—malfunctioning of the computer networks—as the reason.

This move, given the fact that there was no trading at ICE over the following weekend, caused a panic. The banks could not meet the demand from customers, who then turned to the Exchange, which could not do so either. This touched off a general panic that already showed signs of affecting the lari by late Friday evening. The American dollar edged higher, and in most cases, the rate was fixed—but in reality, no one could offer it. ATMs were soon emptied. All these processes were the result of the falling lari.

On Monday, November 10, NBG Acting President David Amaghlobeli said that everything was predetermined and planned, including the timing. The Exchange purposely stopped on Friday, as they had the weekend ahead. Friday, November 7, was the day of the dollar's victory over the lari—an artificially provoked drastic decline—and therefore, this day should be dubbed Green Friday in the annals of modern Georgian history.

If the action was preplanned, as they claim, then Friday was really a very bad time for it, as businesses continued working, unlike government officials. Retail trading occurs on a daily basis. If the government wanted to switch from one rate to another abruptly, it should have done so at the beginning of the week, or at least in the middle of the week—and the NBG administration should have explained its actions publicly the same day.

Moreover, in a TV broadcast on November 8, Zurab Melikishvili, chair of the Parliamentary Committee for Finance and Budget, said that nothing new was happening, and the global financial crisis was ongoing. This confirms that the government did not really plan anything in advance.

So what happened on Green Friday? There are three possible answers:

1. There was a lack of competence and professionalism.
2. This was a deliberate action to allow some people to earn fortunes by speculating.
3. Some people took advantage of the situation to make some money.

I believe that the third answer is most likely true.

What does the future hold for us? Are there any real grounds for a currency crisis in Georgia? There are no economic grounds for a currency crisis; by all accounts, the NBG still has over USD 1.1 billion in its reserves, which would allow a creeping devaluation of the lari. It should be also taken into account that at the donor's conference in Brussels, USD 4.5

billion was pledged in aid to Georgia. Given that this money will come to us over twenty-six months, there is no objective reason that we are in danger of a currency crisis in the coming months or over the next two years.

But the crisis may still worsen; this cannot be ruled out. Unless somebody is held accountable for Green Friday, it may reoccur. Moreover, analysts speculate that, given the artificial shakeups of the rate of the lari, some want to increase it to 1.90 or even 2.00.

If people continue to lose faith in the lari, its decline will become a self-fulfilling prophecy.

8

Postwar Georgia's Economic Challenges

November 26, 2008[*]

After the five-day Russian-Georgian war in August 2008, and in consideration of the global financial crisis, Georgia has come to face new economic challenges. These include, in particular, undoing the economic damage caused by the war, avoiding a crisis in the banking sector, preventing further growth of an already high inflation rate, and preserving the stability of the exchange rate of the national currency: the Georgian lari (GEL). Of no less importance for postwar Georgia is to make a successful transition to the free-trade regime proposed by the United States and the European Union. A timely and adequate

---

[*] V. Papava, "Post-War Georgia's Economic Challenges," *Central Asia-Caucasus Analyst* 10, no. 23, November 26, 2008, https://www.cacianalyst.org/publications/analytical-articles/item/11742-analytical-articles-caci-analyst-2008-11-26-art-11742.html.

response to those challenges will pave the way for Georgia to overcome its present economic hardships.

Background

Generally speaking, the Georgian economy stood the test of the five-day Russian-Georgian war in August 2008, even though it faces considerable difficulties in the aftermath. Direct economic losses consist in ruined settlements and infrastructure, along with considerable environmental damage.

The war threatens Georgia's banking system, as well as the stability of the exchange rate of the national currency, the GEL. August 11 was an especially perilous day for the banking sector; in anticipation of further advancement of Russian occupation forces, individuals and entities started withdrawing their savings and deposits from the banks. In a few days, some half-billion US dollars were withdrawn. In the month following the war's end, only 30 percent of this amount was returned to the banks.

Huge social problems of internally displaced persons (IDPs) from the conflict regions affected by the Russian aggression require government spending. First, the government built temporary homes for those people. These efforts created additional demand for construction materials and labor and may contribute to an economic revival, but with some negative effects. The government's expenses in the construction sector, however essential they may be, will inevitably cause further inflation in a rather short period of time because it is the government, not private individuals or entities, that is buying those homes. Furthermore, the government announced that it will distribute vouchers to IDPs to pay gas and electricity bills, which will add to inflationary pressures. It is true that the government has no choice. But this also makes increased inflation inevitable.

Foreign direct investments (FDI) in Georgia has dropped significantly. The primary reason is that, with the global financial crisis, investors have been trying to make their investments in relatively safer countries. Georgians living abroad have had to reduce remittances to relatives living in Georgia. Considering Georgia's huge foreign-trade deficit (Georgian imports are four times greater than exports), it is no surprise that the GEL exchange rate has become unstable.

The proposed transition to a free-trade regime with the United States and the European Union would encourage a continued flow of FDI into Georgia. Negotiations with the United States are still embryonic, but the EU's conditions are at hand; as decided by the Extraordinary European Council that met in Brussels on September 1, Georgia must meet the conditions of the European Neighborhood Policy. These include the adoption of a new labor code, which would secure for employees the same rights as those protected in the EU, and the enactment of a European-style antimonopoly and consumer-rights protection legislation.

Implications

In October 2008, the donors' conference held in Brussels under the aegis of the World Bank allocated USD 4.5 billion in aid (2 billion in grants and 2.5 billion in loans). Georgia will receive these funds during 2008–2010, and much of it will be spent on undoing the economic damage caused by Russian military aggression.

To avoid a banking crisis, the central bank—the National Bank of Georgia (NBG)—made the right decision when it renewed commercial-bank refinancing, thereby opening a channel of cheap credit resources for the country's commercial banks. At the same time, the basic interest rate on certificates of deposit was reduced from 12 percent to 10 percent (to discourage commercial banks from buying NBG securities), and the minimum reserve requirements for commercial banks were reduced from 15 percent to 5 percent. With these steps, the NBG safeguarded Georgia from a major banking crisis, but at the same time contributed to the growth of money supply—which, in turn, spurs inflation. Having faced a Hobson's choice, the NBG opted for an inflationary rescue, because a banking crisis might have destroyed the economy.

After the war, the IMF, acting within the scope of its standby arrangement, extended USD 750 million, of which 250 million was already transferred to the NBG reserves. Instead of allowing a gradual devaluation of the GEL, the NBG attempted to ensure an almost imperceptible devaluation by effecting regular interventions into the currency market—in one month spending more than USD 300 million of its hard-currency reserves. As a result, the GEL lost only 2.5 percent against the dollar.

However, on November 7, in the Inter-Bank Currency Exchange, commercial banks' demand for dollars soared to more than USD 31 million against a zero supply on their part (as it had been for more than a month before that day). In response, the NBG offered for sale just USD 270,000 and then quit transactions, ostensibly due to technical problems. A general panic ensued: cash machines were cleaned out and currency-exchange outlets drastically raised the dollar exchange rate, with many simply refusing to sell dollars.

The NBG then arranged for a Green Friday. The panic in the currency market continued on Saturday and Sunday as well. On Monday, November 10, when the Inter-Bank Currency Exchange renewed operations, the NBG offered for sale USD 47 million, thereby setting a new dollar exchange rate. Compared to the morning of Green Friday, the lari was devalued by 15 percent. Only then did the NBG leadership make a statement claiming that the events of November 7 had been planned in advance.

Whatever the case, after Green Friday, people have been trying to get rid of GEL, the commercial banks have been reluctant to extend loans in GEL, and the dollarization of the Georgian economy has grown drastically. As imports account for 80 percent of Georgia's consumer market, exchange-rate-induced inflation is one of the most serious economic problems in postwar Georgia.

Although the Georgian government has generally welcomed the EU's initiative regarding the free-trade regime, it has disregarded the EU's conditions. For example, the Letter of Intent sent by the Georgian government to the IMF on September 9 with the Memorandum of Economic and Financial Policies for 2008–2009 avows that in the observable future, the Georgian government does not plan to amend the labor code and adopt new antimonopoly and consumer-rights protecting legislation. So, the Georgian government is by no means hurrying to implement a transition to the free-trade regime with the EU.

Conclusions

In the process of undoing the damage done to the Georgian economy by the war, donors must monitor the spending of all those funds they are giving to Georgia. The spending must be as transparent as possible.

In the aftermath of the war, the devaluation of the GEL was inevitable. However, to maintain the country's macroeconomic stability, it is essential that the devaluation take place gradually, so that any panic in the currency market, like the one that took place on Green Friday, can be avoided. The USD 4.5 billion that Georgia is going to receive in 2008–2010 is a solid foundation for preventing further startling devaluations. However, unless the organizers of Green Friday are held responsible for their decisions and actions, at least politically, similar experiments may be repeated. The restoration of public confidence in the GEL depends on good management of further devaluation.

The transition to a free-trade regime with the EU is of vital importance for Georgia. The Georgian government should not tarnish this issue with political speculation. Up until now, the government provided only intimations that it sought to get closer to the EU. In fact, the government has made no concrete effort to meet EU requirements. In this context, it is of particular importance that the Bretton Woods institutions and the EU closely cooperate and coordinate efforts. Such steps will force the Georgian government to show greater consistency in its actions.

Postwar Georgia Pondering New Models of Development

with Archil Gegeshidze

January 14, 2009[*]

After the August 2008 war with Georgia, Russia unilaterally recognized the independence of Abkhazia and South Ossetia and started setting up its own military bases in both Georgian breakaway regions. As a consequence, a new reality emerged. Unless the status quo of the August 2008 war is restored, Georgia will not only lose all hope for the restoration of its territorial integrity but will face greater difficulties integrating into Euro-Atlantic institutions. Under such circumstances,

---

[*] A. Gegeshidze and V. Papava, "Post-War Georgia Pondering New Models of Development," *Central Asia-Caucasus Analyst* 11, no. 1, January 14, 2009, https://www.cacianalyst.org/resources/pdf/issues/20090114Analyst.pdf.

international experience suggests Georgia must choose a model of development that, on the one hand, will enable the strengthening of regional security and stability, and on the other, will ensure the protection of Georgia's national interests.

Background

Since the early 1990s, the separatist-controlled provinces of Abkhazia and South Ossetia, with the aid of Russia's military and political assistance, succeeded in escaping from Tbilisi's control. Simultaneously, Russia obtained the status of peacekeeper within the CIS format and deployed its "peacekeeping forces" in both regions. In fact, Moscow used these forces to maintain the security of its own puppet regimes.

Although Moscow officially recognized Georgia's territorial integrity when a visa regime was introduced in its relations with Georgia in 2001, it exempted Abkhazia and South Ossetia from the visa regime. That was the Kremlin's first step in politically separating both breakaway regions from the rest of Georgia. Subsequently, residents of both regions were granted Russian citizenship and provided with Russian passports.

After the five-day war between Russia and Georgia in August 2008, Moscow unilaterally recognized the independence of Abkhazia and South Ossetia. It is noteworthy that after a number of Western nations had recognized the independence of Kosovo, the Kremlin did not even attempt to hide its own intentions regarding Georgia's breakaway regions.

Moreover, before the West's recognition of Kosovo, Moscow had repeatedly warned the world that Kosovo would provide a precedent for the recognition of the independence of separatist provinces in the post-Soviet area.

The world's leading nations strongly criticized Moscow's aggression against Georgia and the recognition of the independence of Abkhazia and South Ossetia. Despite this, it is practically unthinkable to expect that in the foreseeable future, Moscow could reverse its decision. On the contrary, Moscow will take steps to keep its military bases there indefinitely. Thus, Georgia has found itself in a situation where it is likely to have a continued territorial dispute with a part of its own territory under occupation. Obviously, Tbilisi will never reconcile with the idea that its territorial integrity has been impaired and that two of its historic provinces have been taken away. The situation resembles something that Europe has experienced a number of times in recent history.

Under the present conditions, Georgia needs to come up with a new model of development based upon international experience that will serve its national interests. From this standpoint, it seems that the cases of Finland, Serbia, and Cyprus are the most relevant to consider. Each of these models has certain strengths and weaknesses.

Implications

Finland's experience is unacceptable to Georgia as a matter of principle. Under enormous military and diplomatic pressure from the Soviet Union, Finland had to make huge concessions in order to preserve its nominal sovereignty. Specifically, in the early 1940s, as a consequence of hostilities conducted in the context of World War II, Finland had to yield 10 percent of its territory to the Soviet Union. Despite the enormous price Finland had to pay for peace, the country managed to maintain a course of political and economic development that made it one of the successful democracies of present-day Europe. This model could figuratively be labeled *stick without carrot*.

For reasons of mentality and historical memory, it is unlikely that Georgian society could reconcile itself with the fact that Abkhazia and South Ossetia are lost for good. The country, then, can make no choice as regards its future development in exchange for the loss of its territories, especially in consideration of the fact that nearly the whole world supports its territorial integrity.

Serbia's example is somewhat different. After February 2008, when the United States and leading European nations did not heed Belgrade's opposition and recognized the independence of Kosovo, Serbia began the accelerated process of integration into Europe. Serbia, as one of the key countries in the Balkans, was practically integrated with the European and the Euro-Atlantic organizations, if this was what it wanted. Furthermore, the EU had already signed a Stability and Association Agreement with Serbia, and talks are underway about the transition to a visa-free regime between Serbia and the Schengen zone.

Becoming European

At the same time, all are aware that without Serbia's recognition of Kosovo's independence, Serbia's integration with the European structures is unthinkable. Consequently, without this, no long-term peace and security may be ensured in the Balkans. In the meantime, even the most pro-Western political groups in Serbia are not ready to lose hope for the reintegration of Kosovo. This is exactly why the West has been trying to drag Serbia into the Europeanization process. The goal is to give Serbia an appetite for the intensification of this process, and so long as it faces this dilemma, eventually to make Serbia give up Kosovo. Again figuratively, this case resembles a *stick with carrot*.

Although Serbia has been promised many carrots for this decision—such as rapid integration with the EU—for the reasons mentioned while discussing the Finnish case, this is a scenario that cannot be reproduced in Georgia.

The example of Cyprus appears to be the most relevant for postwar Georgia. More than thirty years ago, the northern part of the island, with huge Turkish military assistance, broke away from Nicosia, followed by Ankara's recognition of the independence of the Turkish Republic of Northern Cyprus. No other country has followed Turkey's decision since that time.

Meanwhile, strong democratic developments and market-oriented reforms in Cyprus enabled the country to grow in wealth, join the EU, and thereby become attractive to the once separatist-oriented dwellers of Northern Cyprus. In case of eventual reunification of the island, this case would definitely qualify as a *carrot without stick*.

In the twenty-first century, the case of Cyprus might be rather promising for Georgia. The fact is that Brussels' initiatives toward Georgia are not limited to extending financial assistance to Tbilisi. Brussels has announced its readiness for visa facilitation measures within the framework of the Eastern Partnership program and to negotiate a free-trade regime with Georgia, thus making Georgia's Europeanization process increasingly filled with content.

Conclusions

In the aftermath of the Russian aggression against Georgia and Moscow's recognition of the independence of Abkhazia and South Ossetia, the only choice for Georgia is to ensure its democratic development and sound market reforms as prompted by the Cypriot experience. Furthermore, it is recommended that the EU, within the framework of the Eastern Partnership program, tie its political support and financial assistance to Georgia with the latter's success in democratic transformation. This strategy would ensure Georgia's rapid rapprochement with the EU.

The US government, too, has to play an important role in encouraging Georgia to get closer to the EU. To this end, Washington and Brussels must work toward greater coordination of their efforts with respect to Georgia. Harmonizing the US financial assistance to Georgia with the EU's assistance programs would work toward this goal. Making Georgia more EU-oriented should also be a priority for the International Monetary Fund and the World Bank. The conditionality of their programs must be in full harmony with those of Brussels in relation to Georgia.

The New Threats of the Old Cold War

February 18, 2009[*]

Is Europe going to be a battlefield for a new nuclear rivalry? This question became particularly topical after President Dmitry Medvedev of the Russian Federation declared his plans for deploying Russia's Iskander missiles in the Kaliningrad Oblast of the Russian Federation unless US leadership took back its intention to set up a missile shield in Europe. Undoubtedly, this maneuver, especially after the Russian war against the small Caucasus state of Georgia, is reminiscent of the old rivalry between the West and the former USSR in the time of the Cold War. Many politicians and analysts, therefore, ask whether the world is standing on the verge of a new Cold War, and if so, how it could be avoided.

---

[*] V. Papava, "The New Threats of the Old Cold War." *e-politik.de*, February 18, 2009, https://e-politik.de/?p=3247.

Such questions were urgent before Russia's war against Georgia as well. Almost no one, however, is asking the question of whether the twentieth-century Cold War was never finished but rather frozen, and what we are witnessing now is the process of melting.

The West's Dream and Illusion

First in Gorbachev's and later in Yeltsin's epochs, there developed an impression that the Cold War had come to an end and the new Russia had irreversibly chosen a track of cooperation with the civilized world, along with democratic changes and transition to a market economy. Yet the Russian aggression against Georgia in August 2008 made clear that the end of the Cold War was not a reality but, rather, a dream and illusion that the West simply mistook for reality.

In the late 1980s and early 1990s, the collapsing USSR and its successor, a newly independent Russia, were so weak in both political and economic terms that they were greatly dependent upon the West's economic assistance. The desire to get this assistance forced Moscow to turn to the West and Western values. At the same time, nostalgia for the lost empire became increasingly strong in Russia. Many Russians became obsessed with the complex of a beaten nation and the desire to take revenge.

A good example of how the West deliberately turned a blind eye to Russia's antidemocratic actions at times is President Putin's successful enterprise to make his Western partners believe that the Kremlin's war in Chechnya was just an antiterrorist operation. Ironically, the Kremlin accomplished this goal with relative ease, despite a flood of international human rights organizations' criticism that swept Moscow in response to its actions in Chechnya.

In light of the above-mentioned growing revengefulness of Russian society, the military operations in Chechnya drastically increased the Kremlin's esteem inside the country. Coincidentally, this period was marked by a steady growth in oil prices on the global market, which led to a rapid strengthening of Russia's economy. Furthermore, whilst Europe receives 40 percent of its natural gas supplies from Russia, Moscow obtained a powerful weapon that forces the Western world to accommodate the Kremlin. They did so by changing the G-7 format into a G-8 format as a favor to Russia—which, in turn, made the Kremlin believe that it had reobtained enough of its previous influence to dictate its conditions to the rest of the world.

Russia's Growing Influence

It is true that Russia's influence has noticeably grown, but this influence has not been strong enough to dissuade the United States from launching an antiterrorist campaign in Iraq, for example, or to prevent the West from recognizing the independence of Kosovo. These events awakened the Kremlin's passion to show the world that it was much stronger than anyone thought. If the United States is conducting a military operation in Iraq—a country so far away from its shores—then why can't Russia, as one of the leading powers in the world, embark upon a similar action in neighboring Georgia? If many countries of the West recognized Kosovo's independence, then why can't Russia recognize the independence of Abkhazia and South Ossetia—and, thereby, demonstrate to the world that it has truly reobtained its previous power and influence?

Why Georgia?

There comes a further question: why is it that Georgia became Russia's first target? It is not difficult to find an answer.

Firstly, Georgia proper and its two breakaway regions of Abkhazia and South Ossetia have common borders with Russia.

Secondly, both regions have been ruled by Russia's puppet regimes, with their separatism being inspired and fostered politically and economically by the Kremlin, and both of these separatist regimes have been used by Russia as an important base for preparing and implementing a military attack against Georgia.

Thirdly, Georgia's Rose Revolution and Mikheil Saakashvili's government, which came to power as a result of it, have been regarded by the Kremlin as a project of Washington. Furthermore, Georgia's aspirations to NATO have broadly been considered an insult to Russia's national dignity. Finally, Russia wants to dominate pipelines that are crossing Georgia.

Vladimer Papava

The Kremlin's Efforts against Georgia: Past, Present and Future

For quite a long while, the West was unenthusiastic to acknowledge and admit publicly that Tbilisi's key problem in Abkhazia and South Ossetia resided in Moscow. Whilst Moscow was extensively distributing Russian passports in the separatist-controlled regions and persecutions of ethnic Georgians were underway in Russia, the West was still urging the Georgian government to find a friendly settlement with Russia. It was only after Russia launched an act of military aggression against Georgia and occupied the Georgian territories that the Western world realized that Russia was in conflict not only with Georgia but also with Western values.

Euphoric after a quick military victory over Georgia, the Kremlin recognized the independence of both breakaway regions of Abkhazia and South Ossetia and disregarded the fact that the vast majority of the populations in those separatist regions were Russian citizens. Paradoxically, Russia recognized the independence of two new states whose inhabitants were not citizens of Abkhazia and South Ossetia but, rather, and owing to the Kremlin's efforts, of Russia itself. Whilst the Kremlin is fond of drawing parallels with Kosovo, it must be remembered that before recognizing Kosovo's independence, neither the United States nor any other country encouraged the people of Kosovo to accept US or any other country's citizenship.

That the world would not commend Russia for the above steps and would not recognize the independence of Abkhazia and South Ossetia should not be seen as something unexpected

Becoming European

for the Kremlin. Even if some openly anti-Western regimes support Russia's latest moves, they will still be unable to change the climate of modern international relations. There arises another question: What did Moscow count on when it was deciding to recognize the independence of Abkhazia and South Ossetia?

One may foresee that after a certain while, the Kremlin will instruct the puppet governments of Abkhazia and South Ossetia to hold referenda about their incorporation into the Russian Federation. The outcomes of such referenda might be quite predictable, and they could be justified, for example, by the following logic. If the UN, the EU, and most of the world's nations refuse to recognize Abkhazia and South Ossetia, then the people of those states will have no choice but to ask to join with Russia, especially as most of those people are already Russian citizens.

Moreover, Russia is not only a subject of international law but also a permanent member of the UN Security Council. In that capacity, it will be in a better position to protect the interests of the people of Abkhazia and South Ossetia, who will already be inhabitants of the new Russian territories. In so doing, the Kremlin would accomplish objectives that it has been pursuing for a long while, on the one hand, whilst on the other hand being able to successfully blame the West for the extension of Russia's borders into the South Caucasus range because it refused to recognize the independence of Abkhazia and South Ossetia, thereby "forcing" Russia to annex to Georgia's two historical regions.

Vladimer Papava

Conclusion: Refreezing or Completion?

Russia's military aggression against Georgia, the Russian occupation of the Georgian territories, Russia's disrespect for the cease-fire agreement signed by Presidents Sarkozy and Medvedev, and Moscow's unilateral recognition of Abkahzia and South Ossetia without any consultation with the world's leading G-7 nations is naturally reminiscent of the epoch of the Cold War.

To the extent that on both sides of the Cold War are the same countries as in the last century and the reasons and driving forces of the conflict, as well as the Kremlin's action style, have never changed (one must keep in mind that in 2008, the Kremlin made an attempt to replace the political regime in Georgia by the same methods it used in 1956 in Hungary and in 1968 in Czechoslovakia), one may conclude that what we see now is not a new Cold War but, rather, the resumption of the old Cold War. In other words, we are facing the renewal of the same situation that the West mistakenly thought to be over. It appears now that it was just frozen, and the frontline of this melting Cold War is located in the Caucasus, in Georgia.

The political price of Russian gas, notably during the winter (which is the urgent problem of today), is so high that Western European countries, unlike some Eastern European nations that have been exposed to the immediate danger of potential Russian aggression, apparently have chosen to once again turn a blind eye to the reality and Russia's present policy toward the West and Western values. Regrettably, it is quite probable that the old story may happen again, and the West's softness toward Russia may be justified by more self-deceptive assurances that Russia is no longer the USSR and that democratic transformations and Western values are not alien to Russia.

In fact, such an attitude may lead to the renewal of the process of refreezing of the Cold War and the sacrifice of Georgia for an illusory peace in Europe and the whole world. If this is true, then the West's financial and diplomatic support of Georgia may be interpreted such that whilst the West feels an instinctive sympathy for this small country in the Caucasus, by extending this aid it wishes to pay it off. At best, the main challenge for the international community is the elaboration of an effective means for the real—and not virtual, as it was in the late 1980s and early 1990s—completion of the twentieth-century Cold War.

Georgian Economy: Mistakes, Threats, and Resolutions

April 2, 2009[*]

Almost all spheres of the Georgian economy appear to be in a difficult situation associated with high risks that are the consequences of a plethora of mistakes committed in recent years. Moreover, the current situation is significantly and gravely aggravated by Russia's military aggression. The existing threats are seen to seriously hamper a rapid economic rehabilitation of the country in the period following the occupation. The following is a description of the substance of mistakes that have been made in various sectors and ways to prevent them in the future.

---

[*] V. Papava, "Georgian Economy: Mistakes, Threats, and Resolutions," *newcaucasus.com*, April 2, 2009, http://newcaucasus.com/in-english/2008-georgian-economy-mistakes-threats-and-resolutions.html.

Property Rights

Substance of Mistake

The biggest mistake made by the government that came to power after the Rose Revolution is the infringement of property rights. Under pressure from law-enforcement bodies, property owners were forced to surrender their property on a "voluntary basis" for the benefit of the government. This process was conducted under the veil of deprivatization that was supposedly implemented to correct the privatization blunders committed before 2004. In reality, the infringement of property rights was aimed at distributing this property among the so-called elite businessmen standing close to the government. The situation worsened after more than one building was demolished without any legal grounds for doing so, and within which each case was a vivid example of infringement of property rights.

Threats

Infringement of property rights aroused a perception of instability, which is a factor hampering economic growth.

Resolution

An enhancement of the legislative framework for protecting property rights does not suffice. The political will of the authorities is required in order to keep it from happening again.

At the same time, all those whose property was illegally or forcibly expropriated or destroyed should be paid an adequate compensation.

Sale of Public Property

Substance of Mistake

The large-scale privatization process that began in 2004 and went on in full defiance of the law—and bearing in mind the way in which Russian, Kazakh, and Arab capital found their way into the country—is not at all surprising. Frequently, contracts concluded between the government and a new owner exhibited a price that was several times lower than what was announced in the call for privatization.

Quite often, companies with dubious founders and suspicious capital were established just prior to the holding of a tender for the very purpose of participating in the privatization of one or another unit and then emerged as the winners. There were also cases where another state became an owner of Georgian state property, such as Tbilgaz having been transferred into the ownership of a Kazakh state company. This can hardly be considered privatization, even though the government of Georgia did present the transaction as such.

The biggest surprise overall was the nationalization of the privatized United Bank of Georgia by the Russian Federation when the state Russian bank, VneshtorgBank, acquired its control stock following the encouragement of the government of Georgia. The government has publicly rejected the concept of strategic units to be able to sell them freely.

Threats

The lack of transparency in the process of the privatization of state property provides for the possibility of corruption and the transfer of units of strategic importance to Russian companies (including state-owned companies) as an enemy of Georgia whilst enabling further possibilities for economic sabotage in Georgia.

Resolution

The process of the privatization of state property should be made as transparent as possible so that information about the individual company founders is available for all citizens. Further, the law should prohibit the introduction of offshore companies into the Georgian economy. As concerns the units that are presently under the control of Russian capital and companies of suspicious origin (Energo-Pro and Multi-Plex, among others), it is necessary to toughen their public supervision on the part of competent state authorities (the Agency for Financial Supervision, the National Energy and Water Supply Regulatory Commission, and the National Communications Commission) and to have mechanisms for the enhancement of the rights and obligations of these authorities in this direction reflected in the relevant laws.

Vladimer Papava

Limitation of Competition

Substance of Mistake

Following the Rose Revolution, the process of the disruption of public institutions began to facilitate a weakening of Georgian statehood. At the end of 2004, for example, antimonopoly legislation and the state antimonopoly agency were abolished under the suggested reform framework that gave a strong impulse to the emergence of monopolies on the market.

Indeed, it was ridiculous to hear that the president of Georgia had transferred the function of antimonopoly regulation of the market for salt, sugar, and other goods (as reported during a television broadcast of a governmental session in October 2007) to the Ministry of the Interior—even more so given that these commodities have nothing to do with the activities of the police or the State Security Office. Similar and equally ridiculous incidents have taken place in the past, such as the president commissioning the Minister of Defense to seek foreign markets for Georgian wine in 2006.

Threats

The limitation of market competition by monopolies not only impedes economic growth but ultimately causes damage to consumers, who are forced to purchase required goods or services at monopolistically high prices. Furthermore, apart from the disadvantages created for consumers, the absence of antimonopoly regulation presents a serious barrier to Georgia's being granted free-trade regime status by the EU.

Resolution

It is necessary to ensure the adoption and enforcement of a law on antimonopoly regulation that is in compliance with relevant EU recommendations.

State Statistics

Substance of Mistake.

Before 2005, the State Department for Statistics (SDS) was subordinated directly to the president of Georgia, but it was incorporated within the Ministry of Economic Development in 2005, which obviously presents a conflict of interest. As a result, statistics in Georgia today have the same political function as they did in the former Soviet Union; that is, in spite of the actual facts, they must reflect an unconditional yearly improvement of the country's economic situation.

In August 2006, the SDS leaked information that the annual inflation rate was fixed at 14.5 percent as of July. Because of this, the National Bank of Georgia (NBG) and the government of Georgia received severe but deserved criticism from the International Monetary Fund (IMF) permanent representative in Tbilisi. As a result, the chairman of the department was dismissed, and the government appointed another person. who was ordered to make the published inflation rates gradually reduced.

According to the government, the annual inflation rate was set at 8.8 percent as of December 2006 and, therefore, it formally met the IMF's requirement to curb inflation under a two-digit figure. The fact, however, emerged that neither the Georgian people nor experts in the field knew this to be true. Unfortunately, the government continues to manipulate the state statistics with the "successful participation" therein on the part of international financial institutions.

Threats

Biased statistical data fail to provide a more or less realistic picture; therefore, details about the actual situation of the Georgian economy remain hidden from everyone. Falsifying the existing economic data renders the carrying out of appropriate economic policy revision impossible, and continuing to follow this dishonest path is likely to drive the country and its population into very desperate straits.

Resolution

It is necessary to adopt a new law on statistics that will render the respective public authorities truly independent from the government. To this end, it is necessary to remove these institutions from the government with a view to subordinating them to the president or, at worst, the parliament.

The Government Is Stimulating Inflation

Substance of Mistake

Unfortunately, it has become quite typical for our postrevolutionary government to initiate populist economic programs that facilitate the growth of inflation rather than curb it. One of the measures involved in pursuing the noble objective of increasing employment in Georgia asked businessmen to hire an unemployed individual for a three-month term. This individual would be paid GEL 150 per month from the state budget in 2006 and GEL 200 per month in 2007–2008. Tens of millions of lari were spent from state coffers, but few people were actually employed. For many, it simply became a deal with businessmen, who agreed to sign any document stating that a person was in their employ whilst happily receiving a salary for doing nothing at all. There were also reports of businessmen refusing to sign employment documents unless the individual returned half of the money.

In the end, these tens of millions of lari from the national budget were used for the payment of unemployment allowances rather than promoting employment itself. This sum entered the market for the purchase of consumer goods but only stimulated inflation, given that no corresponding volume of goods or services was produced. It should also be noted that a similar program, entitled Clear City, was implemented for students. In addition, vouchers were issued for the purchase of various goods during the winter of 2007–2008, which further contributed to the continued upturn in inflation.

Threats

Such populist programs only succeed in stimulating inflation and generally fail to attain their targets. Apart from making life more expensive for the common people, a high inflation rate undermines macroeconomic stability, which is expected to eventually have a negative effect on the entire economy.

Resolution

The government should express its political will and abandon its unprofessional practice and populism.

Budget Manipulations

Substance of Mistake

Starting in 2008, a new methodology for the formation of the national budget was introduced that led to the apparent disappearance of the phenomenon of a budget deficit. Unused budgetary sums are recorded as surplus over budget expenditure; that is, a budget surplus. In reality, national budget revenues, by their nature, are renewable, and it is for this reason that tax revenues are considered as budget revenues and not one-time incomes. We have a budget surplus; therefore, only in cases when these revenues exceed budget expenditure and we have a budget deficit should they fall below. All one-time revenues, such as proceeds from privatization, grants, or credits, merely represent a source for the coverage of a budget deficit.

Threats

This methodology creates the impression of a national budget surplus, which in fact is far from reality. The budget reflects revenues from privatization, a new foreign debt, and one-time collections, which are clear evidence of a budget deficit. The absence of true information about the national budget's deficiency creates the illusion that the government is pursuing an anti-inflation policy—which, unfortunately, is not true.

Resolution

It is necessary to shift to a universally accepted methodology for the formation of the national budget that will consider only tax revenues—and not one-time payments to the budget—as budget revenues.

Employer-Employee Relations

Substance of Mistake

One of the "achievements" of the postrevolutionary government is the adoption of a version of the labor code that grants maximum rights to an employer while depriving all rights of an employee. The government justifies the establishment of such labor relations by its effort to make Georgia attractive for foreign investors.

In 2006, a presidential initiative envisaged combining the then 20 percent social tax and the 12 percent income tax into a single income tax set at 25 percent. This was accomplished with the new tax change made effective from 2007. Under a decision taken in 2008, however, the income tax rate will be decreased to 20 percent beginning in 2009, which, naturally, is certainly beneficial for employees. We should, however, bear in mind that this tax rate was only 12 percent a few short years ago.

The fact that a social tax and income tax are computed from various tax bases makes it impossible, in principle, to combine them.

Threats

The new Labor Code has further aggravated the social status of the employed. In addition, the absence of any rights on the part of the majority of employees is a serious barrier to the EU granting a free trade regime to Georgia. As concerns taxes, the 20 percent social tax was abolished for employers while income tax for employees increased from 12 percent to 25 percent, which substantially and detrimentally affects their status.

Resolution

In order to regulate labor relations, it is necessary to ensure the adoption and enforcement of a law that will be in compliance with relevant EU recommendations while ensuring a more or less guaranteed security for employees. It would be reasonable to restore the social tax rate at the 12 percent level while reducing the income tax rate to 12 percent in order to equally distribute the tax burden between employers and employees, with a view to reducing both tax rates to 10 percent in the future.

Free Economic Zone: A Trap for Economic Development

Substance of Mistake

The idea of a Free Economic Zone (that is, an economic space wherein, unlike the rest of the territory of the country, various types of tax benefits are applicable) is largely associated with the name of Aslan Abashidze, the former leader of the Autonomous Republic of Ajara. Under conditions of the ongoing economic liberalization in the country, the establishment of a Free Economic Zone seems less expedient as the list of possible tax benefits and their scale are diminishing due to such a liberalization. This argument is essential, but unfortunately, neither Abashidze nor the postrevolutionary government wanted to take it into account.

Threats

The situation is getting even more acute because of the fact that the Georgian economy, during both the prewar and postwar periods, is currently experiencing a lack of investments and, therefore, the creation of a Free Economic Zone under these conditions (as the government decided to do in Poti) would only result in a worse investment hunger on the whole while ultimately hampering the economic growth of the country.

In a situation of investment hunger, both foreign and native potential investors would only put their money in the Free Economic Zone (in this case, in Poti and its adjacent territories) while precluding investing capital elsewhere (such as Kutaisi, Zugdidi, Rustavi, or Telavi, for example), which, therefore, would develop Poti at the expense of the rest of Georgia.

Resolution

The current law on the Special Industrial Zone in Georgia should be abolished. A contract on the establishment and development of a free-trade zone in Poti, as concluded with a selected foreign investor, should be terminated through the taking into account of international practice and upon the grounds that the territory was occupied and damaged by Russian troops during the confrontation in observance of international legal norms.

Weakening of the National Bank of Georgia

Substance of Mistake

The government of Georgia intended to undermine the value of the National Bank of Georgia (NBG) as an independent institution as early as spring 2006 and even prepared changes and amendments to the law on the NBG to this end. Under these changes and amendments, the NBG would lose its bank supervisory function. As a result of this confrontation between the government and the NBG, however, this intention remained unrealized, and the NBG was saved.

In spring 2008, the government took advantage of the resignation of the president of the NBG, at which time his duties were passed to the vice president, to remove the NBG's bank supervisory function despite the resistance of the financial budgetary committee of the parliament. This left the NBG with only one function: to regulate inflation. In addition, the responsibility of the president of the NBG now became dependent upon the upper margin of the yearly inflation rate, which in turn made him dependent upon the government to the extent that it uses various powerful instruments to influence the yearly inflation rate.

Although the IMF stated a request in its memorandum that the government of Georgia preserve the independence of the NBG, it was neglected, given the fact that the IMF was no longer implementing programs in Georgia by the spring of 2008.

Threats

The macroeconomic stability of Georgia is largely dependent upon the activities of the NBG and so limiting its area of regulation to the inflation rate creates a situation for other macroeconomic indicators—such as the exchange rate, balance of payments, and foreign currency reserves—to remain practically neglected. That is, the NBG will consider them only to the extent to which one or another macroeconomic indicators may have an effect upon the annual inflation rate.

As concerns the transfer of the bank supervisory function from the NBG to its subordinate Financial Supervision Agency, the implementation of this function is now fixed at an institutionally lower level, thereby increasing the ability of the government to exert pressure upon this agency. Undermining the institutional value of the NBG makes it more dependent upon the government and more politicized, which ultimately creates a banking system that is less secure while substantially weakening the guarantees of macroeconomic stability.

Resolution

It is necessary to adopt a new law on the NBG in order to increase its independence and diversify its objectives (which should not be limited to regulating the annual inflation rate). This will create a firm guarantee for attaining and maintaining macroeconomic stability. As concerns the bank supervisory function, it is absolutely necessary to return this function to the NBG.

Issuance of Eurobonds and Increasing External Debt by an Additional USD 500 Million

Substance of Mistake

In spite of the fact that national budget revenues were almost continuously on the uptrend after the Rose Revolution, and with the country's leadership having no reason to increase state debt, the government of Georgia nonetheless enabled a growth in its foreign debt by another USD 500 million through the issuance of Eurobonds in April 2008. At the same time, the government has practically admitted that it does not know what the Eurobonds were for.

At first, it was stated that this money was required to finance the construction of energy units, but the government then confessed that half the sum would go to the Future Generations and Stable Development Funds, with a decision regarding the use of the remaining money to be taken at a later date. These particular two funds should be filled by the budget surplus (real and not virtual). Moreover, the government did not even bother to explain the reason for the loan, which taxpayers will have to cover after a period of five years and includes an annual 7.5 percent interest rate.

Following the Russian aggression, the USD 500 million may be used to recover economic losses and for other internal needs of the country.

Vladimer Papava

Threats

Georgia is required to cover its foreign debt by 2013. Under its constitution, parliamentary elections will be held in 2012 and presidential elections in 2013, which makes it very unlikely that a half billion dollars (and even more including the interest accrued) will be found in the national budget to cover this foreign liability. Under such conditions, the government will have to employ the same mechanisms and take a new external loan in the amount required to repay the old one. Given the elections cycle in Georgia, there is high possibility of building up a debts pyramid—that is, a mechanism designed to cover the old liabilities through an almost uninterrupted increasing of new foreign indebtedness that contributes to the unjustified increase in the external liabilities of the country in the long run.

Resolution

It is necessary to make changes to the law of Georgia on the national debt (it may also become necessary to prepare a qualitatively new draft law) which will strictly regulate issues related to increasing the national debt while significantly increasing the responsibility of the government in this sphere to prevent building up a "debts pyramid" in the country.

Green Friday

Substance of Mistake

On Friday, November 7, the demand of commercial banks for the USD exceeded USD 31 million in the conditions of zero supply on the Interbank Currency Market (ICM), with the trend continuing as recently as last month and for more than one month. The NBG could satisfy only USD 270,000 of the demand and then stopped the currency market operations on the basis of technical problems. This resulted in panic that saw ATMs being emptied at once and exchange shops raising the USD rate significantly and often refusing to sell dollars.

As a result, the NBG organized a Green Friday for the country. The panic on the currency market of Georgia continued from Friday through the weekend, with the NBG selling USD 47 million and fixing a new lari rate on Monday, November 10, when operations on the ICM recommenced under which the lari had depreciated by 15 percent against the morning of Green Friday. Only after this did the management of the National Bank announce it had planned the developments of November 7 in advance.

After the war in August, the IMF allocated a USD 750 million credit for maintaining macroeconomic stability in Georgia under the standby arrangement framework of which USD 250 million was transferred to the NBG reserves in the autumn of 2008. Instead of a progressive, creeping depreciation of the Georgian lari, the NBG tried to ensure an almost unnoticeable depreciation of it through the spending of these reserves. Up to USD 300 million was spent from the NBG reserves within one month, which resulted in the lari falling against the USD by only 2.5 percent. Consequently, USD 250 million received from the IMF was spent with a very low result, with the government unable to think of anything better to do than organize Green Friday.

Threats

After Green Friday, the population avoided using the lari, and commercial banks hesitated in issuing credits in lari, which ultimately resulted in a higher dollarization of the economy. Given that 80 percent of the consumer market is accounted for by imports, this gave impulse to a sudden fall in prices.

Resolution

The devaluation of the lari in Georgia was inevitable after the war, but it was necessary in order to ensure that the process of devaluation proceeds at a gradual pace in order to maintain macroeconomic stability and prevent panic on the currency market, as occurred on Green Friday. Assistance to Georgia in the amount of USD 4.5 million in 2008–2010 creates objective grounds for the exclusion of a possible sudden fall of the lari, although it is not excluded that this may happen again if the organizers of this Green Friday do not put forward at least a political responsibility. The process of devaluation should proceed step by step in order to restore confidence in the national currency.

Economic Program

Substance of Mistake

The presidential and parliamentary elections of 2008 proceeded under the slogan "United Georgia without Poverty!" This slogan was embodied by the government in its suggested program under the same title, which was passed by the parliament at the end of January 2008. This document, however, may only conditionally be called a program, to the extent that it is limited to several pages and covered with catchy words and phrases.

It should be noted that a comprehensive National Program on Economic Growth and Poverty Reduction was prepared and approved as early as 2003 by the Georgian president together with the active participation and funding of the IMF, the World Bank, and other international organizations, which at that time earned the high praise of these organizations. The unfortunate fact, however, is that the government, brought to power on a wave of revolution and in its neglect of everything achieved before to the revolution, was so incapable in its activities that there was no attempt to launch the program. Rather, it was consigned to oblivion.

This notwithstanding, both the IMF and the World Bank successfully keep deceiving themselves and publicly declaring their contribution to the program to overcome poverty in Georgia; that is, to something that the government of Georgia itself has not even recognized. Moreover, the IMF even affirmed in September 2007 that the program on poverty reduction in Georgia had been successfully accomplished. Afterward, the government of Georgia had no desire to launch anything new with the IMF, and the Fund would have to wait a long time before it could start another program in Georgia if it were not for the Russian aggression.

Threats

The economic policy pursued recently by the government of Georgia has had no program whatsoever to underpin it. Even the fifty-month or eighteen-month programs that were proposed in 2008 are not accessible and give rise to rather justified doubts about whether or not these documents even exist at all. Meanwhile, the availability of a real economic program creates the grounds to suggest a higher risk of making blunders.

Resolution

The government of Georgia needs to develop a new five-year program on economic growth and poverty reduction and to actively engage and involve both national and international experts from the IMF, the World Bank, and other international institutions in the process.

12

Postwar Georgia: Current Developments and Challenges Ahead

April 2009[*]

Abstract: The postrevolution political regime in Georgia from the very outset was a kind of mixture of democratic and authoritarian elements. After the Russian aggression and under the global financial crises, Georgia is in a more complicated situation. For better understanding the main difficulties and challenges of Georgia, it would be useful to analyze all key tendencies and developments that took place in Georgia after the Rose Revolution and after the Russian-Georgian war. A timely and adequate response to the challenges will pave the way for Georgia to overcome the present hardships.

---

[*] V. Papava, "Post-war Georgia: Current Developments and Challenges Ahead," *Policy Brief ISPI* 127, April, 2009, https://www.ispionline.it/sites/default/files/pubblicazioni/papava_0.pdf.

The Rose Revolution of November 2003 was the outcome of the Georgian people's striving for the development of a democratic society and improvement of human rights. With the passage of two years after the Rose Revolution, the quite natural euphoria that had followed it both inside and outside the country has gradually diminished and been replaced by the state of sobering down that has led to a rather realistic evaluation of the results of postrevolution changes (Papava 2006).

The postrevolution political regime in Georgia from the very outset was a kind of mixture of democratic and authoritarian elements (Nodia 2005). Georgia's experience teaches that a pro-Western and an anti-Russian orientation is by no means a firm and adequate guarantee of democracy (Papava 2008a). While to many politicians in the West the crushing of the peaceful demonstrations in the Georgian capital, Tbilisi, in November 2007 appeared to be totally unexpected and, consequently, shocking, for analysts, these events were more or less predictable (Mitchell 2008). After the five-day Russian-Georgian war in August 2008, and in consideration of the global financial crisis, Georgia has come to face some new economic challenges (Papava 2008b).

The Splendor and Misery of Postrevolution Georgia

Georgia's government inherited from the Shevardnadze administration numerous unsolved problems from which one should distinguish the following: energy crisis and budgetary crisis (meaning that because of the inability and unwillingness of public officers to collect taxes, the government accumulated huge arrears of pensions and salaries in the public sector). Most of such problems were conditioned first of all by a high degree of corruption.

From the moment of his coming to power, Mr. Mikheil Saakashvili set a goal to concentrate powers in the president's hands. The lack of any more or less critical remarks with respect to the presidential power reinforcing developments on the West's part stimulated further growth of authoritarian tendencies in the public governance (Areshidze 2007, 197–295). It is hoped that the West will no longer blindly trust Georgia's president and parliament (Applebaum 2008).

The strengthening of presidential powers in Georgia had some positive implications in terms of establishing financial order in the country, accomplishing some significant increases in tax revenues, and, as a consequence, overcoming the above-mentioned budgetary crisis. Among some other accomplishments of the postrevolution government, one should emphasize the qualitative improvement of the criminological situation in the country. The strengthening of presidential powers enabled the government to start an effective fight against corruption. In this context, one must mention the abolition of traffic police that had existed since the Soviet times, as well as the creation of a Western-style patrol police in a very short period of time.

The combat of corruption in the energy sector resulted in the overcoming of an energy crisis. As of the winter of 2006–2007, all of Georgia has been enjoying about a 100 percent supply of electricity. Among the postrevolution government's accomplishments, one should also emphasize the introduction of national examinations for admission to universities, which replaced the old corrupt system of separate admission exams in individual universities that had existed since Soviet times.

A fourfold growth of the national budget revenues was achieved as a result of such anticorruption measures as arresting and releasing former government officials and their relatives for a "price of liberty." Officially, this was proclaimed as paying back to the state money and properties that had been stolen from it (McDonald 2005). Such revenues cannot be raised on a regular basis. At best, they can be collected one more time and with much less effect. The government, specifically for this purpose, established extrabudgetary "law-enforcement development accounts" where those suspected of corrupt practices were compelled to transfer payments to buy their liberty.

The launch of a large-scale privatization program should also be regarded as one of the key accomplishments of the postrevolution government. Deregulation, such as reducing the number of licenses and permits, has limited the legal grounds for government's interference with businesses. Cutting tax rates significantly eased the tax burden for businesses. Reducing the import-tax base for agricultural produce and construction materials as well as the annulment of the import taxes for other goods has made Georgia much more competitive.

The new labor code was revolutionary. By limiting the rights of employees, it has substantially broadened those of employers. Although this may encourage businesses to develop, it also leaves employees unprotected.

After the publication of the World Bank's rating list in 2006 entitled "Doing Business," according to which Georgia had made an impressive jump from 112th to 37th place among the world's nations, the Georgian government announced that its next year's objective would be to push the country forward and to ensure that Georgia would be found among the twenty best nations of the world in the World Bank's rating list. In fact, it did assume eighteenth place in 2007 and fifteenth place in 2008 (WB 2009).

Among the negative consequences of strengthened presidential power, one should distinguish an intensified feeling of impunity among government officers that, in the first place, has been manifested in a gross disrespect for the rule of law. Humorously, the significantly weakened parliament is often called the "government's notary." As to the judiciary, it has become an appendix to the general prosecutor's office and the whole executive branch (Anjaparidze 2006a). The government's control of media and, most of all, of TV channels has become overwhelming (HRIDC 2008a).

One has to emphasize the ways of transformation of corruption in postrevolution Georgia. The extrabudgetary accounts, which used to accumulate income from accused persons' paying the "price of liberty," has been described above. Because such accounts were outside the budgetary area, it is natural that there was no transparency in terms of spending. However, the problem became even more serious as the government started replenishing those accounts by means of so-called voluntary contributions from businesses (Anjaparidze 2006b). Later, in the spring of 2006, under the IMF's pressure, the extrabudgetary accounts were abolished.

The postrevolution government's disrespect for the constitution and laws became evident in the process of the privatization of public property. By means of bypassing the law, or much rather in its complete defiance, some new owners started to emerge from nowhere.

The process of deprivatization launched after the Rose Revolution is another reason for concern. Deprivatization in the context of postrevolution Georgia means that certain objects that had been privatized before the revolution were forcibly taken back by the government, which then offered them again for privatization. In the process, the law-enforcement organs (the general prosecutor's office and the Ministry of the Interior) got involved, pressuring owners to "voluntarily" give up their property for the government's benefit. The government seemed not to be concerned at all that property rights were grossly infringed upon (HRIDC 2008b).

Against the background of a successful fight with mass corruption, there still remains unsolved the problem of elite corruption involving high-level government officers who, on the one hand, in defiance of public procurement regulations, with total impunity, have been using budgetary resources for their own benefits, and, on the other hand, have been exploiting their official status to protect their favorite companies under their umbrella.

Into the context of the above-described negative consequences of the postrevolution government's activities do fit quite well multiple violations of human rights (including murders of young people by policemen for which, as is broadly believed by the public, not all responsible persons received fair punishment (HRIDC 2004, 2007).

Whither Russia?

In postrevolution Georgia, integration into Russia's economic domain has become prominent (Papava 2008c). In 2003, Anatoliy Chubais, president of the management board of RAO EES (Unified Energy Systems) Russia and prominent Russian statesman and political figure, wrote that Russia should establish a "liberal empire" in the post-Soviet world (Chubais 2003). It would be liberal in the sense that the new empire should be based on economics rather than coercion, wherein Russian companies (public and private) would take over the ownership of strategic companies in the former Soviet republics that, in the long run, must lead to the reestablishment of Moscow's political control.

The first step toward snaring Georgia in the liberal empire's net was the summer 2003 takeover of the shares of the US-based company Road by RAO EES. The Georgian government fully supported the entry of Russian capital into the Georgian economy during the large-scale privatization of government-owned enterprises after the Rose Revolution. The best example was the sale of Georgian gold and copper mining and processing companies to Stanton Equities, a subsidiary of the Russian holding group Industrial Investors. Encouraged by the government's affinity for Russian capital, the owners of the United Georgian Bank (privatized in 1995) sold it to Russia's Vneshtorgbank, of which 99 percent is owned by the Russian government. This sale was the nationalization of the United Georgian Bank by the Russian government.

The strangest thing is that even after the Russian-Georgian war in August 2008, President Saakashvili is still welcoming Russian business activity in Georgia (Bedwell 2009). Regrettably, it is evident that Georgia is being pulled into Russia's liberal empire (Papava and Starr 2006).

Supersaturated 2008

In November 2007, to rescue his own image as well as that of Georgia, President Saakashvili resigned and called for an extraordinary presidential election for January 5, 2008. On May 21, 2008, a parliamentary election was carried out. During both campaigns, it was apparent that Mr. Saakashvili and his party were using administrative resources for their own interests. The elections were competitive, considering the circumstances, and polling was mostly uneventful.

In the final accounting, Mr. Saakashvili received slightly more than the 50 percent required to avert a runoff, whilst the National Movement now controls 80 percent of the seats in the parliament. International observers gave qualified approval to the campaign environment and elections conduct, but they also have mentioned serious reservations about using administrative resources and about the ballot counting (OSCE 2008a, 2008b). It can be inferred that during the presidential and parliamentary elections, the government implemented several large-sized projects the economic viability of which is doubtful to a greater extent (Lashkhi, Evgenidze, Narmania, and Gabedava 2008).

In August, Russia started military aggression against Georgia (Antonenko 2008; Cornell 2008; Jones 2008). Generally speaking, the Georgian economy stood the test of the five-day Russian-Georgian war in August 2008, even though it has to deal with a number of considerable difficulties in the aftermath of the conflict (Kakulia 2008).

At the conference held in Brussels under the aegis of the World Bank in October 2008, it was decided to allocate USD 4.55 billion in financial aid for postwar Georgia, of which USD 2 billion is a grant and the remainder a loan. Georgia will receive these funds during 2008–2010, and a major part will be spent for the liquidation of economic damage caused by the Russian military aggression. The process of spending must be as transparent as possible.

The problem that has appeared in the aftermath of war is that the inflow of foreign direct investment in Georgia has dropped significantly. The primary reason is that investors have been trying to make their investments in relatively safe countries under the conditions of the present global financial crisis, rather than ones like Georgia, which was seriously affected by the recent Russian aggression. The global financial crisis drove Georgians living abroad to reduce their financial aid to relatives living in Georgia. Add to this the country's huge foreign trade balance, where imports exceed exports by four times, and you will see that it came as no surprise that the stability and exchange rate of the national currency, the lari, were shattered.

The proposed transition to the free trade regime with the EU can be a very important factor for encouraging the continued flow of foreign investment into Georgia. The transition to the free trade regime, as was decided by the Extraordinary European Council that met in Brussels on September 1, 2008 (CEU 2008), is dependent upon Georgia's meeting those conditions which Brussels has requested to be observed within the format of the EU Neighborhood Policy. These include the adoption of a new labor code that would secure the same rights for the employees as are protected in the EU itself and the enactment of European-style antimonopoly and consumer-rights protection legislation.

Although the Georgian government has generally welcomed the EU's initiative regarding free trade, the EU's conditions, which are considered a must by this organization, regrettably have hitherto been disregarded by the Georgian government. The Memorandum of Economic and Financial

Becoming European

Policies for 2008–2009 with the IMF (IMF 2008) makes any impression that in the observable future the Georgian government plans to amend the labor code and adopt a new European-standard antimonopoly and consumer rights protecting legislation questionable. Up to now, the government has just pretended that it was striving to get closer to the EU.

Hot Spring of 2009

In addition to the Georgian government's mistakes, the country's people have been greatly disappointed by the Georgian president's falling into Russia's trap in August 2008, when he renewed hostilities in South Ossetia and eventually brought about Georgia's defeat in the war with Russia. In late August 2008, Moscow recognized the independence of Abkhazia and South Ossetia, even though Nicaragua is the only country in the world that has supported this step. Remarkably, Russia has deployed and further strengthened its military bases in both of the occupied regions.

The rigged presidential and parliamentary elections, the lost war with Russia, and other serious mistakes committed by the government have paved the way for another great wave of protests inside the country. President Saakashvili has been opposed by his closest allies and team members, such as Irakli Okruashvili, the former defense minister; Nino Burjanadze, the former speaker of the parliament; Zurab Noghaideli, the former prime minister; Irakli Alasania, the former ambassador to the UN; and Erosi Kitsmarishvili, the former ambassador to Russia. All but Kitsmarishvili have become leaders of their own new political parties. In concert with the other nonparliamentary opposition groups, they have demanded President Saakashvili's resignation and called for an extraordinary presidential election. With these demands, they have planned to organize nonstop rallies and manifestations, which will start on April 9, 2009 (a day commemorating the restoration of Georgia's independence). According to them, the protests will only finish when the president steps down.

It is noteworthy that a demand to replace Saakashvili has also been repeatedly articulated by the Kremlin during the August 2008 war, as well as since its end. In this context, nothing can be easier than to accuse the opposition of fulfilling the Kremlin's orders. The government has constantly claimed that the opposition has been driven by Russia's undercover agents. Moreover, in every step taken by the opposition, the government sees traces of the northern neighbor. Such a situation raises doubts that by its constant demands to replace the president, the Kremlin actually aims to weaken the Georgian opposition and give Saakashvili another chance to stay in office.

The leaders of the opposition have made repeated promises that the protests will be exclusively peaceful. With the approach of April 9, however, the government has intensified its live-on-TV arrests of some opposition party members, ostensibly for their illegal trade in firearms. These television shows have made many people believe that the government has deliberately deployed its undercover weapons dealers with the opposition groups to generate a terror of civil war among the Georgian public.

It looks like Georgia is facing another serious test. The key question is whether the country will be able to overcome a political crisis by democratic means or if it will continue moving in the direction of authoritarianism. The spring of 2009 will be a time for measuring Georgia's success or failure as a democracy.

Conclusions

The postrevolutionary government initially showed the political will to establish financial order and eradicate the bribery that allowed the country to overcome the budgetary and energy power crises. At the same time, the government made numerous mistakes along its revolutionary road, among which the repeated violations of property rights bear a repeated highlight. An authoritative ruling does not allow President Saakashvili and the ruling party to recognize and correct the mistakes made during the postrevolutionary period.

By no means of less importance for Georgia, however, is the postwar period. The challenge is that Georgia does not slide toward the Russian model of a so-called controlled or sovereign democracy under which the Russian leadership has attempted to hide its authoritarian rule. The West's role in this respect is indispensable.

References

Anjaparidze, Z. 2006a. "Critics Press for Improved Judicial Independence in Georgia." *Eurasia Daily Monitor, The Jamestown Foundation*, 3, 81, April 26, https://jamestown.org/program/critics-press-for-improved-judicial-independence-in-georgia/ (last accessed April 10, 2009).

Anjaparidze, Z. 2006b. "Georgian Government Questioned about Secret Funds." *Eurasia Daily Monitor, The Jamestown Foundation*, 3, 71, April 12, https://jamestown.org/program/georgian-government-questioned-about-secret-funds/ (last accessed April 10, 2009).

Antonenko, O. 2008. "A War with No Winners." *Survival*, 50, 4: 23–36.

Applebaum, A. 2008. "Getting Past Mythmaking in Georgia." *Washington Post*, November 20, http://www.washingtonpost.com/wp-dyn/content/article/2008/1 1/19/AR2008111903533.html (last accessed April 10, 2009).

Areshidze, I. 2007. *Democracy and Autocracy in Eurasia: Georgia in Transition*. Michigan: Michigan State University Press.

Bedwell, H. 2009. "Georgia's Saakashvili Won't Impede Russian Business." *Bloomberg*, March 13, http://www.bloomberg.com/apps/news?pid=20601095&sid=a4lxHDlgb19M&refer=east_europe (last accessed April 10, 2009).

CEU. 2008. "Extraordinary European Council, Brussels, 1 September, 2008, 12594/08." *Presidency Conclusions*, Brussels: Council of the European Union, http://www.con silium.europa.eu/ueDocs/cms_Data/docs/pressData/en/ec/102545.pdf (last accessed April 10, 2009).

Chubais, A. 2003. "Missia Rossii v XXI veke [Russia's Mission in the 21st Century]." *Nezavisimaya gazeta*, October 1, http://www.

ng.ru/printed/ideas/2003-10-01/1_mission.html (last accessed April 10, 2009).

Cornell, S. E. 2008. "War in Georgia, Jitters All Around." *Current History*, 107, 711, October, pp. 307–14, http://www.silkroadstudies.org/new/docs/publications/2007/0810CH.pdf (last accessed April 10, 2009).

HRIDC. 2004. *One Step Forward, Two Steps Back. Human Rights in Georgia After the "Rose Revolution."* Tbilisi: Human Rights Information and Documentation Center, http://www.humanrights.ge/files/REPORT.pdf (last accessed April 10, 2009).

HRIDC. 2007. *Georgia: A Flickering Beacon of Democracy; Human Rights in Georgia in 2007*. Tbilisi: Human Rights Information and Documentation Center, http://www.humanrights.ge/admin/editor/uploads/pdf/Annual%20Report%20HRIDC%202008.pdf (last accessed April 10, 2009).

HRIDC. 2008a. *Putinization of Georgia: Georgian Media after the Rose Revolution Media in Georgia 2003–2007*. Tbilisi: Human Rights Information and Documentation Center, http://www.humanrights.ge-/admin/editor/uploads/files/Georgian%20Media%20after%20the%20Rose%20revolution.pdf (last accessed April 10, 2009).

HRIDC. 2008b. *The Big Eviction. Violations of Property Rights in Georgia*. Tbilisi: Human Rights Information and Documentation Center, http://www.humanrights.ge/admin/editor/uploads/files/Big%20Eviction.pdf (last accessed April 10, 2009).

IMF. 2008. *Georgia: Letter of Intent, Memorandum of Economic and Financial Policies, and Technical Memorandum of Understanding, September 9, 2008*. Washington, DC: The International

Monetary Fund, http://www.imf.org/External/NP/LOI/2008/geo/090908.pdf (last accessed April 10, 2009).

Jones, S. F. 2008. "Clash in the Caucasus: Georgia, Russia, and the Fate of South Ossetia." *Origins: Current Events in Historical Perspective*, 2, 2, http://ehistory.osu.edu/osu/origins/article.cfm?articleid=20 (last accessed April 10, 2009).

Kakulia, M. 2008. "Mitigating Post-War Economic Threats in Georgia." *Georgian Economic Trends*, October, http://www.geplac.org/newfiles/GeorgianEconomicTrends/2008/October%202008%20(eng).pdf (last accessed April 10, 2009).

Lashkhi, I., N. Evgenidze, D. Narmania, and M. Gabedava. 2008. *The "50-Day Program" of the Government of Georgia: Analysis and Conclusions*. Tbilisi: Open Society Georgia Foundation Policy Paper, 15.

McDonald, M. 2005. "Democracy Flourishes a Year After Georgia's Rose Revolution." *Knight Ridder Washington Bureau*, March 8, http://www.accessmylibrary.com/comsite5/bin/pdinventory.pl?pdlanding=1&referid=2930&purchase_type=ITM&item_id=0286-84696 21&word=Democracy_Flourishes_Year (last accessed April 10, 2009).

Mitchell, L. 2008. "What Was the Rose Revolution For? Understanding the Georgian Revolution." *The Harvard International Review*, February 27, http://www.harvardir.org/articles/1684/ (last accessed April 10, 2009).

Nodia, G. 2005. The Dynamics and Sustainability of the Rose Revolution, in M. Emerson, ed. *Democratisation in the European Neighbourhood*. Brussels: Centre for European Policy Studies, http://www.uquebec.ca/obser vgo/fichiers/57785_1267.pdf (last accessed April 10, 2009).

OSCE. 2008a. *Georgia. Extraordinary Presidential Election, 5 January 2008. PSCE/ODIHR Election Observation Mission Final*

Report, March 4 2008. Warsaw: OSCE, http://www.osce.org/docum ents/odihr/2008/03/29982_en.pdf (last accessed April 10, 2009).

OSCE. 2008b. *Statement of Parliamentary Findings and Conclusions. International Election Observation Mission. Georgia - Parliament Elections, May 21 2008*. Tbilisi: OSCE, http://www.osce.org/documents/odihr/2008/05/31268_en.pdf (last accessed April 10, 2009).

Papava, V. 2006. "The Political Economy of Georgia's Rose Revolution." *Journal of World Affairs – Orbis*, 50, 4, http://www.fpri.org/orbis/5004/papava.georgiaroserevolution.pdf (last accessed April 10, 2009).

Papava, V. 2008a. "Georgia's Hollow Revolution. Does Georgia's Pro-Western and Anti-Russian Policy Amount to Democracy?" *The Harvard International Review*, February 27, http://www.harvardir.org/articles/1682/1/ (last accessed April 10, 2009).

Papava, V. 2008b. "Post-War Georgia's Economic Challenges." *Central Asia-Caucasus Analyst*, November 26, http://www.cacianalyst.org/?q=node/4991 (last accessed April 10, 2009).

Papava, V. 2008c. "The Essence of Economic Reforms in Post-Revolution Georgia: What About the European Choice?" *Georgian International Journal of Science and Technology*, 1, 1: 1–9.

Papava, V., and F. Starr. 2006. "Russia's Economic Imperialism." *Project Syndicate*, January 17, http://www.project-syndicate.org/commentary/papava1 (last accessed April 10, 2009).

WB. 2009. *Doing Business. Economy Rankings*. Washington, DC: The World Bank Group, http://www.doingbusiness.org/EconomyRankings/ (last accessed April 10, 2009).

# 13

Myths about the Georgian Economy

October 18, 2011[*]

During the reforming of postrevolutionary Georgia's economy, significant experience has been accumulated in this field, both positive and negative. A plethora of myths about postrevolutionary Georgia have been created. The most accepted myths about Georgia's economy need to be debunked.

Myth 1: Georgia—A Country of Neoliberal Reforms

Georgia received this status thanks to the enumerated successes in reforming its economy. Adoption of a labor code that limits

---

[*] V. Papava, "Myths about the Georgian Economy," *Democrarcy & Freedom Watch*, October 18, 2011, https://dfwatch.net/myths-about-the-georgian-economy-11211-860.

Becoming European

employees' rights and expands those of employers should be pointed out, along with a downsizing of government employees, reduction of the tax burden, and simplification of procedures for obtaining licenses and various types of permits necessary for starting up a business. Such reforms were called *neoliberal reforms*. It was emphasized that such reforms would contribute to making the country more attractive for investment.

Thanks to these reforms, *Doing Business*, which is prepared by the International Financial Corporation (IFC) and the World Bank, moved Georgia from 112th place to 37th place in 2006; to 18th place in 2007; and to 12th place in 2010. Of course, the government of the country advertises this achievement in every way possible. The actual situation is not as cheerful as the results of the rating may suggest.

After the Rose Revolution, there were many cases of infringement of property rights in Georgia, especially those of Georgian entrepreneurs. Private owners "voluntarily" gave up the rights to their property due to pressure from the law-enforcement ministries, or private buildings and facilities were demolished without a court ruling. In many cases (but not always), the government is cautious with regard to foreign investors, as they have the ability to attract attention to their problems from outside Georgia's borders. Also taking into account the absence of a judicial power independent from the political elite of and gross interference by the government in private business and in general the violations of human rights, it can be confidently confirmed that the government does not hold back from applying certain neo-Bolshevik methods in the economy.

Given this explosive mixture of neoliberal rhetoric and the neo-Bolshevik essence of the economic reforms, the above-mentioned *Doing Business* rating strongly overestimates Georgian reality. In our opinion, any rating must be read with caution, as the result of the rating very much depends on the methodology with which stakeholders are interviewed in order to obtain a qualitative assessment of an event.

This can be easily proven if, for comparison, we refer to the data of the Global Competitiveness Report 2010-2011 rating prepared by the World Economic Forum. According to this rating, the situation in Georgia is far from perfect. In its overall rating, Georgia lands at 93rd place; concerning ownership rights, it ranks at 116th place; when it comes to independent judicial power, it is at 104th place; and in terms of effectiveness of antimonopoly policy, Georgia ranks at 135th place.

What gives a more adequate view of the economic condition in the country is not various ratings but statistical information, which confirms that Georgia's citizens are in quite a difficult situation. Even by official data, 20 percent of Georgia's population is living below the poverty level, and 60 percent are below the median consumption level (i.e., consumption of an average household). According to experts' evaluation, 86 percent of the population is experiencing serious social difficulties.

Myth 2: Georgia—A Country Free of Corruption

After widespread combat against corruption immediately after the Rose Revolution, which led to success in the budgetary sphere, electricity sector, and patrol police, there emerged a myth, not without the government's participation, that the country had become completely free of corruption.

It is true that widespread petty corruption has been minimized. But the situation with regard to elite corruption, which transformed from simple bribing into more complex forms, is far more complicated. However strange it might seem, active combat against corruption contributed to this. Specifically, when former high officials and their relatives, who were suspected of corruption, paid a ransom (or "price of liberty") for their freedom, those payments did not go solely to the national budget. Extrabudgetary accounts were established at the law-enforcement bodies (state prosecutor's office, Ministry of Internal Affairs, and Ministry of Defense) immediately after the Rose Revolution, and a part of the payments were channeled to those accounts. As no one exercised monitoring over those accounts, it is not known how much money was accumulated and how those funds were spent.

It is obvious that such measures as collection of ransom in return for the person's freedom have only a one-time effect. In the best case, it can be used again, but with lesser results. Thus, the businessmen were forced to make contributions to those accounts. Only after this did the IMF ask the government of Georgia to abolish such funds. The government agreed to do so, but not immediately.

The practice of "voluntary" contributions by businesses at the request of the government is a characteristic component of postrevolutionary corruption schemes. The deprivatization process, or a review of results of privatization and repeated privatization, started in Georgia after the revolution. Through intimidation, the law-enforcement ministries made owners of privatized enterprises "voluntarily" give up their property the government. As for the privatization, this process might be characterized as nontransparent, which provides fertile soil for corruption.

Myth 3: Georgia—A Country with a European Orientation

Georgia was not hiding its pro-Western orientation even before the Rose Revolution, but this became more obvious in the postrevolution period. Aspiration to NATO was especially emphasized. The ambition to join the EU was not hidden either.

Brussels has made significant steps toward establishing and deepening cooperation with some post-Soviet countries, including Georgia. Thus, Georgia has been closely cooperating with the EU under the European Neighborhood Policy since 2004, under Black Sea Synergy since 2007, and within the framework of Eastern Partnership since 2009. Officially, Georgia actively promotes its European orientation. But when it comes to making actual steps, the decisions of the government are inadequate, to say the least.

Thus, after the Russian-Georgian armed conflict of August 2008, already on September 1, 2008, the Extraordinary European Council held a meeting in support of Georgia, and

Georgia was offered the Deep and Comprehensive Free Trade Agreement (DCFTA) for free trade with the EU—provided Georgia meets certain conditions necessary for uniting the economic areas. Specifically, Brussels asked Tbilisi to adopt European-type antimonopoly legislation (antimonopoly regulations were abolished after the Rose Revolution) and food-safety legislation (which was suspended after the revolution), and to amend the labor code so that the rights of employees are protected.

Though Tbilisi welcomed this suggestion from Brussels, after several days, the government of Georgia signed a memorandum with the International Monetary Fund (IMF) committing itself to not undertake these institutional reforms in the near future. It is well-known that the IMF mainly focuses on maintaining macroeconomic stability, and the World Bank deals with institutional reforms. Thus, we can infer that a clause in the memorandum was initiated by the government of Georgia, not the IMF.

Only in 2011 did the food-safety regulations became effective again, and discussions regarding preparation of draft antimonopoly law have just started. Discussions about amendments to the labor code have not started yet.

At the same time, the government of Georgia has become more and more fascinated not by the West but by the East. First of all, the government is attracted to Singapore's experience, as well as that of Dubai and Hong Kong. According to President Saakashvili, Georgia's economy must be developed using the Singapore model. "The European track" is at best mentioned in passing reference, such as "Georgia must become Switzerland with Singapore elements." This ignores significant differences among economic models as well as institutional arrangements of these countries, to say nothing of the fact that Singapore's model is unlikely to be useful for Georgia and that such developed countries do not combine well with the declared European choice. The government of Georgia further moves the country away from the EU and generally from the European types of economy by taking the path of Singaporization.

In gambling on Singapore's example to become a country that has a government with authoritarian features, the government of Georgia underlines the neoliberal character of its economy and, almost as importantly, the absence of the regulations that Brussels requires from Tbilisi for introducing a free-trade regime. Such views regarding Singapore's economy are removed from reality, as this country has fully operating food-safety institutions as well as antimonopoly regulations. It must be noted that the president of Georgia's interest in the so-called Singaporization of the economy (and of the whole country) is shared by the president of Belorussia.

Some positive expectations are connected with the Joint Declaration of the Warsaw Eastern Partnership Summit (September 29–30, 2011), according to which the EU could start talks with Georgia on DCFTA by the end of 2011, "provided sufficient progress has been made in fulfilling a number of remaining key recommendations."

14

Russia's Accession to the WTO: The Perspective from Tbilisi

December 2011[*]

Current Situation

In Geneva on November 9, 2011, Georgia and Russia ended years of talks by signing an agreement on Russia's accession to the World Trade Organization (WTO). Georgia, a WTO member, had been willing from the outset to agree to Russia's accession provided that customs checkpoints could be opened on the Abkhaz and South Ossetian sections of the border with Russia. This condition was based on the principle that

---

[*] V. Papava, "Russia's Accession to the WTO: The Perspective from Tbilisi." *International Alert*, December 2011, https://www.international-alert.org/blogs/russias-accession-wto-perspective-tbilisi.

movement of goods on the borders of two neighboring states must be subject to national customs legislation.

At that point, the Kremlin had not yet recognized Abkhazia and South Ossetia as independent states. Thus, the Abkhaz and South Ossetian sections of the border with Russia were recognized by Moscow as forming part of the Russian-Georgian border.

The situation was further complicated following the five-day war between Russia and Georgia in August 2008 and Moscow's subsequent de facto unilateral recognition of Abkhazia and South Ossetia as independent states. In Moscow's view, economic (and not only economic) relations between Russia on the one hand and Abkhazia and South Ossetia on the other were seen as international relations between two states. This view had been maintained regardless of the reaction from Tbilisi, international organizations, and most countries around the world.

The Georgian administration has not, on the whole, changed its prewar position on Russian accession to the WTO. Moscow treats Tbilisi's conditions on this issue as purely politically motivated, although the Georgian side has emphasized that these requirements fall squarely under the heading of trade relations that require cross-border trade between the trading states.

The agreement reached in Geneva has not gone down well in Abkhazia and South Ossetia. This is because it involves locating international observers on the border with Russia to monitor cross-border trade. Abkhazia and South Ossetia have viewed this as impinging on their sovereignty (RFE/RL 2011). However, Moscow has officially stated that this agreement between Georgia and Russia does not impinge on the independence of Abkhazia and South Ossetia (MID 2011).

Significance of WTO Membership

An important point to make here is that Russia has been trying to become a WTO member since 1993. Although the average length of time needed to become a member is six years, it has taken Russia three times as long. This is mostly due to inconsistencies in the government's actions on WTO membership (Åslund 2010). These inconsistencies were probably also fueled by economic skepticism over Russia's accession to the WTO based on a rough cost/benefit analysis. This analysis suggested that the benefit to Russian companies of WTO accession would be a maximum of USD 23 billion versus potential losses of up to USD 90 billion once foreign companies enter the Russian domestic market (Rubchenko and Koksharov 2006).

On the other hand, a significant argument in favor of WTO membership for Moscow was that Russia, as a G8 country, should be a member, since the WTO is a major international organization whose member countries together account for over 95 percent of global trade. Russia was also the only remaining G20 country not to be a WTO member. In other words, it was politically unacceptable for Russia, which justifiably sees itself as a global leader, to be outside a global organization that directly sets the rules on global trade.

Even from an economic perspective, Moscow is clearly keen to be involved in setting international trade rules, given that WTO member countries account for 92 percent of Russia's trade. This is a further motivation behind Russia's special interest in WTO membership. Another serious consideration for Moscow is the high probability that accession to the WTO would lead to the United States repealing its Jackson-Vanik amendment, which Moscow finds humiliating (Gwertzman 2011).

The Crucial Issue

The talks process on Russia's accession to the WTO—and to an even greater extent, the agreement reached with Georgia—once again confirms the reality that Russian interests may not always and in every detail coincide with the interests of Abkhazia and South Ossetia. This is entirely natural, given the difference in size of the countries as well as Russia's international significance (Markedonov 2011). At the same time, however, Moscow is keen to defend the independence of Abkhazia and South Ossetia now that it has recognized them.

Switzerland's mediation in the talks process between Georgia and Russia was an opportunity for both countries to reach agreement. It provided a chance to discuss and reach an agreement on proposals by a third party, Switzerland, which offered a compromise. This solution involves locating monitors from a private certified company specializing in customs operations to be recommended by the Swiss side. The monitors are to be located on the Russian side of the de facto border with Abkhazia along the Psou River and the de facto border with South Ossetia at the northern point of the Roki Tunnel, as well as at the Kazbegi-Upper Lars checkpoint on the Georgian military highway that connects Georgia and Russia through North Ossetia without entering South Ossetia.

Under this solution, the disputing parties are free to put their own construction on the situation according to their interest in Abkhazia and South Ossetia. It allows Tbilisi to take the view that setting up a standardized monitoring procedure at customs points along the Abkhaz and South Ossetian borders with Russia and also at the Kazbegi-Upper Lars checkpoint represents indirect recognition by Moscow that the border between Georgia and Russia coincides with Russia's borders with Abkhazia and South Ossetia. On the other hand, since the monitoring procedure at the customs points along the border between Russia and Abkhazia and South Ossetia and at the Kazbegi-Upper Lars checkpoint is also standardized, Russia can take this to mean that there is a standardized procedure covering all three of its equally independent (in its view) neighbors: Abkhazia, Georgia, and South Ossetia.

A distinction should be made between Abkhazia and South Ossetia. This relates to the fact that the agreement reached between Georgia and Russia relates solely to land borders, even though trade between Russia and Abkhazia also goes by sea.

Maritime borders between Russia and Abkhazia are not subject to monitoring by international observers. This is an option that is not open to inland South Ossetia. Air borders between Russia and Abkhazia will also not be monitored. However, Abkhazia's airports are only designed to receive passenger and military transport flights.

Although monitoring of cross-border trade is an additional barrier to international trade, it is important to note that this barrier applies not just to Abkhazia and South Ossetia but equally to all three of the checkpoints. However, following the import ban introduced by Moscow in 2006 on Georgian agricultural products and the relative diversification of Georgia's external trade links (for example, recently created new export markets for Georgian wine), this new barrier is not likely to be the cause of any particular additional difficulties for Tbilisi. South Ossetia is set to be the greatest loser, since all its external trade is with the Russian Federation and conducted solely by land. Abkhazia is in a slightly better position, partly because the barrier does not cover its maritime trade with Russia, but also because Russia accounts for just two-thirds of Abkhazia's external trade. Its second largest trading partner is Turkey, with which it trades by maritime routes.

In our view, the introduction of a customs monitoring mechanism may well bring significant benefits for the entire region. This would be mainly due to the significant curtailing of contraband flows, although at this stage, this cannot be quantified. An important consideration is that following Russia's accession, WTO rules will apply to the majority of countries in the region, since Armenia and Turkey are members as well as Georgia. This will create a sound legal basis for the development of regional trade based on WTO trade conflict resolution mechanisms. The WTO will provide the institutional framework necessary for growth in trade, although membership in itself is not a sufficient condition for increasing trade.

Conclusion

The agreement between Georgia and Russia to install international monitors at checkpoints does not extend to the maritime and air borders of Abkhazia and Russia. These checks on overland trade in goods will create an additional barrier to trading with Russia for all the entities they cover. This will affect Abkhazia to a lesser extent than South Ossetia, since it trades with Russia by land and sea and Abkhazia has a further trading partner in Turkey. At the same time, the talks process between Georgia and Russia on Russia's accession to the WTO has once again been a lesson to the Abkhaz and South Ossetians, demonstrating that they must learn to live with the hard fact that Moscow is not always and in every detail able or willing to consider their interests. This is something not yet realized by those involved, whether in Sukhumi and Tskhinvali on the one hand or Tbilisi on the other.

One undisputed positive aspect of employing international observers to monitor cross-border trade could be the significant curtailment of contraband flows in the region. Moreover, trade relations in the region are likely to be boosted once the majority of countries in the region (Armenia, Georgia, Turkey, and soon Russia too) are members of the WTO. This will also indirectly benefit Abkhazia, whose maritime and air borders with Russia are not subject to international monitoring.

References

Åslund, A. 2010. "Why Doesn't Russia Join the WTO?" *The Washington Quarterly*, April, http://www.twq.com/10april/docs/10apr_Aslund.pdf (last accessed November 21, 2011).

Gwertzman, B. 2011. "Impact of Russia's WTO Entry on U.S." *The Council on Foreign Relations*, November 10, http://www.cfr.org/russian-fed/impact-russias-wto-entry-us/p26473 (last accessed November 21, 2011).

Markedonov, S. 2011. "Vstuplyenie v VTO: Abkhazskoye i yugo-osetinskoye izmereniye [WTO Accession: the Abkhazian and South Ossetian Dimension]." *POLITKOM.RU*, November 10, http://www.politcom.ru/12858.html (last accessed November 21, 2011).

MID. 2011. "MID RF: Protokol po VTO ne ushchemlyaet nyezavisimosti Abkhazii i Yuzhnoy Osetii. [MID of the RF: Protocol on WTO does not Impinge on the Independence of Abkhazia and South Ossetia]." *REGNUM*, November 10, https://regnum.ru/news/1465809.html (last accessed November 21, 2011).

RFE/RL. 2011. "Abkhazia, South Ossetia Alarmed by Russia-Georgia WTO Compromise." *Radio Free Europe/Radio Liberty*, November 8, https://www.rferl.org/a/abkhazia_south_ossetia_

alarmed_russia_georgia_wto_compromise/24384963.html (last accessed November 21, 2011).

Rubchenko, M., and A. Koksharov. 2006. "Zaderzhis na poroge [Pause on the Threshold]." *Ekspert*, November 6, https://expert.ru/expert/2006/41/shans_prodat_rossiyskie_rynki_podorozhe/ (last accessed November 21, 2011).

15

Democracy: A Goal or Merely a Commitment for the West?

May 21, 2012[*]

It is a widely held view that a major goal of Western powers is the strengthening of democratic processes in every country of the world. The basis for such a view is the recognition that the West, namely the United States and the EU, furnishes excellent examples of democratic arrangements and have publicly declared priorities of building and developing democracy. In my opinion, however, recent developments have shown that this is not necessarily always the case. Much more significant for the West is that the country's government will be sympathetic and willing to offer support (whether political, military, or economic).

---

[*] V. Papava, "Democracy: A Goal or a Merely a Commitment for the West?" *openDemocracy*, May 21, 2012, https://www.opendemocracy.net/en/odr/democracy-goal-or-merely-commitment-for-west/.

Becoming European

Being pro-Western, of course, does not always mean sharing the democratic values that are recognized and established in Western countries. Usually, being pro-Western means supporting the political and economic interests of the West in a given country and in the neighboring region. It is by no means unacceptable for the West to cooperate with authoritarian regimes (not to mention dictators) in different countries. Obvious examples from recent years are the warm relations of the USA with Hosni Mubarak in Egypt; of France with Ben Ali in Tunisia; or of Italy with Muammar Gaddafi in Libya.

If undemocratic regimes are not pro-Western in the sense described above but the states they govern are relatively big and, therefore, considerable powers, the West nonetheless tries to maintain firm and steady relations with them. Western calls for strengthening democracy in such countries tend to be more ritual in nature than targeted at actual outcomes. China and Russia belong to this class of state for the West. It is, therefore, hardly unsurprising that leaders of Western democratic governments saw fit to congratulate Vladimir Putin on being elected president for the third time and, by so doing, effectively offer him their support.

Those undemocratic regimes, which are more or less well aware that strengthening democratic processes is not a decisive factor for the West, try to satisfy the West's major political and economic interests and to assist with the realization of these interests in their countries and in the neighboring regions.

Vladimer Papava

Democratization: A Process of Backing the Winner

The Arab Spring offered a very interesting recent example. The undemocratic regimes in power were under Western protection, but as soon as growing popular protest was clearly becoming irreversible, Western leaders felt compelled to turn their backs on these regimes and take the side of the people. That said, neither Paris nor Washington was in any hurry to turn its back on Ben Ali or Hosni Mubarak, respectively, when the protest rallies started. In the Arab countries, it was only large protest rallies that reminded the West about democracy. This allows us to conclude that for the West, democracy is more of a stated commitment than a real goal.

If a pro-Western but undemocratic regime manages to maintain its power in such a way as to prevent protest rallies or to keep them few and far between, then support for the democratic process in that country is not a Western priority. If, however, the people can no longer endure the undemocratic regime and express their ever-increasing readiness to overthrow it, then the West recalls its main commitment and takes the side of the rebels in support of democracy.

The Arab Spring should have been a valuable lesson for the West, and the failure to pay attention to it was a serious mistake. Specifically, the commitment of the West to support democracy should be more important than allowing countries to adopt pseudo-Western status, and the criteria for deciding whether a government is pro- or pseudo-Western must be radically changed. Only those governments that do their best to support democratic values and the irreversible strengthening of the democratization process above all else should be considered pro-Western.

Elections in Georgia: Yet Another Test for Western Democracy

Whether or not the West has learned its lesson from the Arab Spring will become clear in the course of the autumn 2012 parliamentary elections in the post-Communist state of Georgia. President Mikheil Saakashvili's regime came to power as a result of the Rose Revolution (BBC 2005) in November 2003. Initially, it cultivated a reforming democratic image, but this was revealed to the world as false on November 7, 2007, when the government brutally broke up a protest rally (BBC 2007). The authoritarian character of Saakashvili's regime has, over the years, become increasingly apparent: the abuse of human rights is systematic, property rights are flagrantly violated, the judiciary is subordinate to the government, and freedom of speech is restricted.

All this time, however, the West has attached more importance to the fact that the leader of Georgia was trying his best to be an outpost for the West (more specifically, for the USA) in the Caucasus. For the West, and especially the USA, the significance of governments in countries bordering Iran being avowedly pro-Western is paramount, and Mr. Saakashvili uses this to strengthen his regime.

On every possible occasion, Mikheil Saakashvili has attempted to prove his devotion to the USA. Georgia sent military troops to Iraq and Afghanistan. In Afghanistan, Georgia makes the biggest contribution of the non-NATO member countries participating in the International Security Assistance Force. At the same time, several famous lobbyist companies are engaged in promoting the pro-Western image of President Saakashvili.

In 2013, Saakashvili's second term as president expires. Changes to the Georgian constitution initiated by the president will enable him to maintain his position in the country. The next leader of Georgia will be a prime minister, rather than president, elected by Parliament for an unlimited term of office. It is vitally important for President Saakashvili that his party, the National Movement, triumphs at the 2012 parliamentary election, as this will allow him to assume the post of prime minister.

Georgia will thus become the new testing ground for the West. To put it a different way, what is more important: a goal to maintain the regime of a so-called pro-Western but really pseudo-Western Saakashvili, or a real commitment to protect the main democratic principles and not allow him to rig the coming elections and prevent the usual street protests and rallies? We shall very soon find out which one the West opts for.

References

BBC. 2005. "How the Rose Revolution Happened." *BBC News*, May 10, http://news.bbc.co.uk/2/hi/4532539.stm (last accessed April 30, 2012).

BBC. 2007) "Tear Gas Used on Georgia Protest." *BBC News*, November 7, http://news.bbc.co.uk/2/hi/7082317.stm (last accessed April 30, 2012).

16

The Kremlin and Georgia: Collusion or Illusion?

July 24, 2012[*]

In the autumn of 2011, a Georgian billionaire called Bidzina Ivanishvili set up his own political party to oppose the undemocratic regime of President Mikheil Saakashvili. Georgia's ruling party, the National Movement, immediately denounced him as a "project of the Kremlin"—an accusation that is very harmful for Georgia.

This claim needs to be understood in its historical context. Since Georgia won its independence twenty years ago, Georgians have been in the habit of examining their political leaders for evidence of Kremlin sympathies. On these grounds, perceptions of Georgia's first two presidents vary.

---

[*] V. Papava, "The Kremlin and Georgia—Collusion or Illusion?" *openDemocracy*, July 24, 2012, https://www.opendemocracy.net/en/odr/kremlin-and-georgia-collusion-or-illusion/.

Becoming European

Zviad Gamsakhurdia, Georgia's first president, was accused by his opponents of having yielded to KGB pressure in the 1970s and "repented his anti-Soviet activities." However, during his presidency, relations with Russia became very tense and subsequently broke down completely.

The second president, Eduard Shevardnadze, was similarly criticized. He stood accused of having availed himself of Russian help, first to topple the government of his predecessor, then to maintain his position as head of state when Gamsakhurdia's armed forces tried to restore the democratically elected government. He remained vulnerable to this charge despite the fact that retrograde forces in Moscow had never forgiven Shevardnadze for his contribution to the collapse of the Soviet Union.

Fevered suspicion of Kremlin sympathies is hardly surprising, given that for almost two hundred years, Georgia was part of the Russian and subsequently Soviet Empire. It has always been vitally important for Georgians, as no doubt for citizens of other post-Soviet countries, to be sure that their leader is not a Kremlin project. Such suspicions, it must be admitted, all too often arise from oversensitivity. These so-called insidious Kremlin plans all too often turn out to be a phantom.

However, the issue of Kremlin influence on Georgian politicians is not just a major concern for Georgians but also for foreigners with an interest in the country. In the case of Bidzina Ivanishvili, it was not difficult for the Saakashvili propaganda machine to work on the anxieties of some foreigners and encourage them to spread the rumor that Ivanishvili was working for the Kremlin. However, foreign specialists with a better knowledge of Georgian domestic issues were more cautious and skeptical of the wilder claims put about by the propaganda machine.

Is Barack Obama (or Nicolas Sarkozy) a Kremlin Project?

It was Barack Obama who first advanced the idea of resetting US relations with Russia on the grounds that an improved understanding between the two countries could only lead to an improvement in relations. So the question as to whether the US president was a Kremlin project has some place in the post-Soviet context.

Obama is now coming to the end of his first term, and it is clear that the reset has not worked. Indeed, some specialists even claim that it has had the opposite effect to the one desired. In their view, Moscow, seeing the initiative as a sign of weakness, was motivated to harbor unrealistic geopolitical ambitions. Russia has further intensified its anti-Western stance, as can be seen from the statements and actions of Vladimir Putin. Barack Obama's reset idea is, of course, a function of his (and his team's) naiveté rather than of any Kremlin sympathies.

Nicolas Sarkozy was similarly suspected by some in Georgia of being part of the Kremlin project. France was EU president in the second half of 2008, and in this capacity, Sarkozy tried to bring the hostilities of the Russo-Georgian war to an end and find a way out of the impasse. He achieved a degree of success in this, though Moscow has still not fulfilled all its obligations; indeed, Russia has violated the terms of the agreement by recognizing the independence of the occupied territories of Abkhazia and South Ossetia. President Sarkozy had little to say on this subject and subsequently even sold a Mistral helicopter carrier to Moscow. So perhaps Sarkozy could have been a Kremlin sympathizer too.

Is the simple fact that the heads of some big countries attempt to improve their relations with Moscow sufficient evidence for them to be dubbed Kremlin sympathizers? The answer is more complex than it might at first appear. Let us consider the facts behind the charge laid against Ivanishvili.

The Boundary between Reality and Fantasy

What grounds do Mikheil Saakashvili and his supporters actually have for accusing Bidzina Ivanishvili of being a Kremlin project? Is it just that he made his billions in Russia and a significant part of his business interests are based there?

Ivanishvili was particularly vilified for holding 1 percent of shares in the Russian energy giant Gazprom. Saakashvili and his team did not seem to mind this when they were accepting donations from him before he went over to the opposition. These donations went to projects for the government of Georgia. Sometimes the projects were even in the name of Saakashvili's ruling party, the National Movement. But when Ivanishvili decided to join the opposition, he was immediately denounced as a Kremlin sympathizer, spending his billions to serve the interests of Moscow.

Such arguments could be turned against Mikheil Saakashvili himself. Perhaps he is a Kremlin project? The facts do not look too good. Members of the opposition frequently refer to the fact that the young Saakashvili served in the USSR KGB's border forces from 1989–90. So he could well have started working for the KGB in the final years of the USSR.

Saakashvili and his supporters especially do not like to be reminded of the role Igor Ivanov played in Georgia's Rose Revolution. On November 23, 2003, the tension in the center of Tbilisi had reached a peak when Russian Foreign Minister Ivanov paid a special visit to the capital and appeared at the opposition rally in support of the revolutionaries. From there, he went to a meeting with the president, after which Shevardnadze announced his resignation, effectively bringing the Rose Revolution to an end.

In 2004, Igor Ivanov played an equally important part in the Ajara revolution (BBC 2011) when Saakashvili attempted to reimpose the authority of the central government on this autonomous region. On May 5, in his capacity as secretary of the Security Council of Russia, Ivanov arrived in the Ajaran capital, Batumi. At dawn on May 6, he left for Moscow, taking with him Aslan Abashidze, chairman of the Supreme Council of the Ajara Autonomous Republic and his son, Giorgi.

Clearly, the Kremlin was not at the time against Mikheil Saakashvili becoming leader of Georgia in place of Eduard

Shevardnadze. Indeed, Russia even played its part in ensuring that he did.

After the Rose Revolution, Mikheil Saakashvili opened the doors wide to Russian investment in Georgia, thus facilitating Georgia's gradual entry into the web of Russia's liberal empire (Papava and Starr 2006), publicly announced by Moscow. Saakashvili's government supported the handing over to Russian companies of large Georgian industrial and energy companies. The privately owned United Georgian Bank was nationalized by the government of the Russian Federation when its Vneshtorgbank (VTB) acquired a controlling interest in the bank. The Georgian government also intended to sell Gazprom, the main north–south gas pipeline (RFE/RL 2010), which was built in Soviet times and runs from Russia through Georgia and into Armenia. Luckily for the Georgians, however, that deal fell through when Washington became involved in the project.

After the Rose Revolution, Kakha Bendukidze (Economist 2004), an ethnic Georgian millionaire from Moscow, was invited to become the leader of the Georgian government's economic team. He created a bridge between Russian business and the Georgian government. Mikheil Saakvashili was unconcerned by the fact that, before he arrived in Tbilisi, Bendukidze had been chairman and CEO of the United Heavy Engineering Group OMZ. This company produced equipment for the nuclear energy industry, meaning that the CEO would have been likely to be in close touch with the Russian security services. The Georgian president and his supporters are also not keen to be reminded that Saakashvili, by his own admission, telephoned President Putin to confirm Bendukidze's appointment with him.

Not even the war in August 2008 put a stop to the inflow of Russian investment into Georgia. Indeed, when the war was over, the Russian telecommunications company Beeline increased its activities. In 2011, the Georgian government sold two hydroelectric plants to Inter Rao, one of the largest Russian public energy companies, and issued a license for the construction of three new plants. In the summer of 2012, President Saakashvili nominated Ivane Merabishvili, a former interior minister, as the new prime minister of Georgia (RFE/RL 2012). Just two months earlier, Mr. Merabishvili had declared in Parliament that "money doesn't smell" and that he welcomed Russian investments in Georgia.

Perhaps it even suits the Kremlin to have Saakashvili as head of state in Georgia? The very fact that Moscow refuses to have any official relationship with Tbilisi gives the Russian president a free hand to do what he wants in occupied Abkhazia and South Ossetia. It is no coincidence that Moscow has decided to conduct military exercises in the North Caucasus in the autumn of 2012, at the time of the Georgian parliamentary election. In so doing, the Kremlin is reinforcing President Saakashvili's claims that Russia might once more attack Georgia, thus fanning nationalist feeling and increasing the number of his supporters at the elections.

Is there a boundary between reality and fantasy? There are the facts. There are, however, those who refuse to believe them. That is their choice.

References

BBC. 2011. "Regions and Territories: Ajaria." *BBC News*, November 22, http://news.bbc.co.uk/2/hi/europe/country_profiles/3520322.stm (last accessed July 15, 2012).

Economist. 2004. "A Different Sort of Oligarch." *The Economist*, July 29, https://www.economist.com/business/2004/07/29/a-different-sort-of-oligarch (last accessed July 15, 2012).

Papava, V., and F. Starr. 2006. "Russia's Economic Imperialism." *Project Syndicate*, January 17, https://www.project-syndicate.org/commentary/russia-s-economic-imperialism?barrier=accesspaylog (last accessed July 15, 2012).

RFE/RL. 2010. "Georgia's Main Gas Pipeline Up for Grabs." *Radio Free Europe/Radio Liberty*, July 9, https://www.rferl.org/a/Georgias_Main_Gas_Pipeline_Up_For_Grabs/2095528.html (last accessed July 15, 2012).

RFE/RL. 2012. "Georgia's Siloviki in the Ascendant." *Radio Free Europe/Radio Liberty*, July 13, https://www.rferl.org/a/georgia-siloviki-on-the-rise/24644540.html (last accessed July 15, 2012).

Spiegel Online. 2012. "Georgian Billionaire Bidzina Ivanishvili: 'I Am the Last Free Man in This Country'." *Spiegel International*, March 27, https://www.spiegel.de/international/world/interview-with-georgian-billionaire-bidzina-ivanishvili-a-823925.html (last accessed July 15, 2012).

17

US Elections: Hopes and Expectations from a 'Post-Rosy' Georgia

October 23, 2012[*]

Georgia's parliamentary election of October 1 signified the beginning of the end for the authoritarian regime of Mikheil Saakashvili, who was swept into power by the Rose Revolution in November 2003. For a long time, President Saakashvili exploited PR techniques and his oratorical gifts to preserve his image as a post-Soviet democrat and reformer. At the same time, there was a dawning recognition for many that his government's abuses of human rights and property rights, and its unofficial control of business and the media, were

---

[*] V. Papava, "US Elections: Hopes and Expectations from a 'Post-Rosy' Georgia," *openDemocracy*, October 23, 2012, https://www.opendemocracy.net/en/odr/us-elections-hopes-and-expectations-from-post-rosy-georgia/.

Becoming European

very familiar, resembling Bolshevik excesses from the Soviet past. The authoritarian-style government was reinforced with elements of despotism—a frequent topic of conversation in mid-September after the publication of shocking video footage filmed in Georgian prisons (Elder 2012)—made the Saakashvili regime neo-Bolshevik and his government rosy in two senses: it was the Rose Revolution that brought him to power, but it also harked back to the red of the Bolsheviks.

The election that brought billionaire Bidzina Ivanishvili (Harding 2012) and his opposition coalition Georgian Dream to power may have been contested, but it was not fair: the rosy government made maximum use of its management reserves as well as finances from the national budget, while at the same time vetoing Ivanishvili using his own money to fund his election campaign. Despite this, the winner of the election was the Georgian people, who have a strong desire to live in a democratic country where their human rights will not be abused—where there is freedom of speech and the market economy will have a chance to develop. The Georgian Dream victory in the election marks the beginning of a new stage of development, which we might call post-rosy.

But for Georgia—as, indeed, for the whole world—the results of the US presidential election are far from unimportant. America is the main strategic partner of this small nation in the Caucasus, so the question is not simply one of idle curiosity.

Vladimer Papava

Rosy Georgia: Attitudes to the Republican Candidate

In May 2005, the Republican US president, George W. Bush, came to Tbilisi. The whole of Georgia was delighted, because his visit was generally regarded as confirmation of Washington's support for Georgian independence. This obvious endorsement was regarded by President Saakashvili as a license to deviate from the generally accepted standards of a democratic society.

It was after the American president's visit to Tbilisi that Saakashvili's rose government started becoming increasingly like its Soviet predecessor. Georgians were amazed to see that the Bush administration preferred to look the other way as Saakashvili gradually abandoned democratic ideals, and the general perception of America as the flagship of democracy began to fade. Georgia was nevertheless grateful to the Bush administration for its support at the time of Russian military aggression in August 2008.

During the 2008 US presidential election, Georgia's rose government and its supporters were openly rooting for the Republican candidate, John McCain. The hope was that Washington would then continue the Bush policy of blind support for the increasingly authoritarian Saakashvili regime. For exactly the opposite reason, the rest of Georgia supported the Democratic candidate, Barack Obama, in the hope that he would not be encumbered by the obligations of his Republican predecessor.

Post-Rosy Georgia: Attitudes toward the Democratic Candidate

The Georgian Dream victory at the polls can be laid first and foremost at the door of the Georgian electorate, which on the whole resisted government subornation and was unafraid of the rosy regime's punitive measures. Voters were properly appreciative of the efforts made by the United States, the EU, and several international organizations during the election campaign, the election itself, and afterward.

Worthy of special attention was President Obama's statement after his January 2012 meeting with President Saakashvili (CG 2012) about the need for a peaceful transfer of power after the election. Secretary of State Clinton also spoke about this on more than one occasion with the Georgian leadership.

Georgian voters were particularly struck by the fact that the day after the election—and long before the formal announcement of the results—US Ambassador Richard Norland and US senators Jeanne Shaheen and James Risch congratulated the leader of the Georgian Dream coalition, Bidzina Ivanishvili, on his victory at the polls. It was only after this that President Saakashvili accepted his party's defeat. Previously he had officially stated that his party, the National Movement, would retain its parliamentary majority. In diplomatic language, this means that Mikhail Saakashvili was under pressure from Georgia's American friends to accept things as they were—that is, defeat—in order to preserve his image as a democrat.

It was very important for Georgian citizens who triumphed at the polls that the American Democratic administration endorsed the choice of the people rather than the so-called pro-Western, but nondemocratic, Saakashvili, who had received such blind support from the Republican administration. It goes without saying that everyone who voted for Georgian Dream wants to see Barack Obama reelected as president of the United States. They are not at all sure that Saakashvili, with the assistance of his Republican friends, would not manage to get the support of Mitt Romney should he be elected.

This perception of Democrats and Republicans in the United States somewhat simplifies the reality, of course, which is evidenced by the fact that Bidzina Ivanishvili received his first congratulations from the Democrats (Senator Jeanne Shaheen) and the Republicans (Senator James Risch). President Saakashvili will stay in the post for one more year, until the next presidential election. Acknowledging his party's defeat at the polls, he declared that he was going over to the opposition, although what this actually means is still not quite clear.

Fears are periodically expressed in Georgia that Saakashvili and his team will take revenge, although for the moment, there are no objective grounds for this apprehension. But recent bitter experience has taught the Georgians to hope that the Americans will elect the Democratic candidate as president.

When Bidzina Ivanishvili appeared on the political scene and set up his Georgian Dream party, many Georgians became dreamers. Among their dreams is the hope that their country will truly be able to move toward democracy. They also hope that their country's main strategic partner will have an administration that will offer realistic support for their chosen course of democratic development and will not turn a blind eye to any deviation from it, however insignificant.

References

BBC. 2005. "How the Rose Revolution Happened." *BBC News*, May 10, http://news.bbc.co.uk/2/hi/4532539.stm (last accessed October 15, 2012).

CG. 2012. "Obama Meets Saakashvili." *Civil Georgia*, January 31, https://old.civil.ge/eng/article.php?id=24399 (last accessed October 15, 2012).

Elder, M. 2012. "Georgia Prison Guards 'Captured on Video Torturing Prisoner'." *The Guardian*, September 19, https://www.theguardian.com/world/2012/sep/19/georgia-prison-guards-torture-video (last accessed October 15, 2012).

Harding, L. 2012. "Bidzina Ivanishvili: The Eccentric Billionaire Chasing Georgia's Leadership." *The Guardian*, October 1, https://www.theguardian.com/world/2012/oct/01/bidzina-ivanishvili-profile-georgia (last accessed October 15, 2012).

18

Georgia's Socioeconomic Development: Prospects over the Medium Term

December 16, 2012[*]

The Tortuous Path of Economic Reforms in Post-Soviet Georgia

Georgia's economy has undergone huge changes since the country reclaimed its independence over twenty years ago. The initial years of independence were particularly difficult, when the country was engaged in armed conflict and had no coherent economic policy to speak of. Serious mistakes were made, particularly in the initial stages of the transition from

---

[*] V. Papava, "Georgia's Socio-Economic Development: Prospects over the Medium Term," *International Alert*, December 16, 2012, https://www.international-alert.org/blog/socio-economic-development-english.

Becoming European

a command economy to a market economy. The cumulative effect of these mistakes was that, by 1993, the country's gross domestic product (GDP) was 30.73 percent of the level in 1990. Annual inflation stood at over 7.84 percent in 1994.

In 1995, a currency reform was successfully implemented, allowing macroeconomic stability to be achieved, along with a rise in GDP of almost 24 percent in 1996–1997. However, the negative impact of the 1998 Russian default on Georgia's economy, together with the resulting spread of corruption, exacerbated the country's existing budget and energy crises. By 2003, more than half (52 percent) of the Georgian population had an income below the official poverty line.

After the Rose Revolution in November 2003, a fight against corruption was launched and the budget and energy crises were overcome. Since 2005, a new tax code has reduced the tax burden significantly, while procedures for registering business start-ups have been considerably simplified. In addition, new labor legislation has been passed giving employers complete freedom of action in relation to their employees. These reforms have portrayed Georgia as a country of neoliberal reforms.

However, there were also many documented instances of violations of property rights, and big business came under the complete control of the government. Moreover, the abolition of antimonopoly legislation and its regulatory body created an economy that was dominated by monopolies. Despite the disappearance of mass corruption—mainly in the form of bribery—elite corruption has started to assume threatening proportions. These crimes represent a kind of neo-Bolshevism, and Georgia's present-day economy represents a symbiosis of neoliberalism and neo-Bolshevism.

In the years since independence, Georgia has managed to establish itself as a transit corridor linking Europe with Asia. Major oil and gas supply pipeline projects have been completed.

After the August 2008 Russia-Georgia war, the European Union expressed its willingness to grant Georgia a free-trade regime, setting a number of preconditions. The most important of these preconditions are the implementation of European-style antimonopoly market regulation and the introduction of consumer-rights protection, particularly in the area of food safety. Unfortunately, the Saakashvili government did all it could to postpone the start of talks with the EU by delaying implementation of these conditions.

In early 2009, the United States–Georgia Charter on Strategic Partnership was signed, under which the United States acknowledged the possibility of the United States concluding a free trade agreement (FTA) with Georgia. However, there has been little real movement on this so far, and negotiations have not even begun.

The Georgian Economy: In Search of a Development Model

Unfortunately, the contemporary Georgian economic model is based less on increasing production and more on stimulating consumption. This model has led to many negative consequences.

Stimulating consumption while ignoring the need to develop the real sector of the economy has led to the country importing four times as much as it exports. Of its exports, 22 percent is motor cars and 8 percent is scrap metal. However, Georgia has no car-manufacturing industry: this 22 percent share of exports is due to Georgia's function as a transshipment point, importing motor cars for resale to neighboring countries. The significant gap between exports and imports, combined with the fact that 30 percent of Georgia's exports are not produced by the real sector of the economy, indicates the relative economic backwardness of the country.

In total, government and private consumption accounts for around 90 percent of GDP. This is further evidence that the Georgian economy is more oriented toward consumption than production. The relative backwardness of the manufacturing sector means that this increase in consumption has been funded by flows of monies from abroad. In the first years after the Rose Revolution, this was mainly in the form of foreign direct investment (FDI) and remittances to Georgian citizens from relatives living abroad.

FDI mostly went into real estate, creating a new financial resource within the country. This financial resource, mediated mainly through the banking system, sparked a housing boom, which without appropriate government regulation soon turned into a financial pyramid scheme.

Since independence, many residents of Georgia have for various reasons left the country. At present, around 20 percent of the population of Georgia (more than 1 million people) is living abroad (two thirds of them in Russia, but also in Greece, Turkey, Ukraine, the United States, and Spain, among other countries). Remittances sent through banks alone amount to over USD 1 billion per year. This money is mainly used to meet basic needs.

Given the low level of savings, the main source for maintaining and increasing the funds available for lending at commercial banks was borrowing on the European financial markets. This once again provided credit for building and for purchasing home appliances. Since home appliances are not produced in Georgia, however, this led to a situation where consumer borrowing from Georgia's commercial banks promoted the development of the real sector of economies in the countries that produce these goods. In other words, the banking sector in Georgia acted as a conduit for foreign loans that provided credit to develop the real sector of economies in third countries. The increased capital flows into Georgia following the Rose Revolution thus created a new demand without enabling the development of the manufacturing sector to meet it.

With the start of the global financial crisis, FDI in Georgia fell sharply. A further factor in this was the Russian-Georgian war in August 2008. Georgia, as the victim in this war, received USD 5.8 billion in financial assistance from the international community. As a result, the impact of the global financial crisis on Georgia was relatively mild.

Unemployment levels are relatively high as a result of the backwardness of the real sector of the economy. According to official statistics, the level of unemployment is over 15 percent. However, a number of sociological surveys of the population, carried out by local and foreign nongovernmental organizations, state that 70 percent of those questioned consider themselves to be unemployed. The main reason for this is that over 55 percent of the workforce is self-employed and their incomes are so low that they do not view this work as employment.

Over 80 percent of the self-employed work in agriculture. More than half (54 percent) of the workforce is employed in the agriculture sector, but agricultural production accounts for just over 8 percent of GDP. Given that Georgia's natural and climatic conditions are excellent for agriculture, this is evidence of an agricultural crisis of underproduction. It also explains why 80 percent of basic food products are being imported. Georgia's agriculture sector has also suffered from the ban announced in 2006 by the chief public sanitary inspector of Russia on the importing of agricultural products from Georgia due to their allegedly low quality.

Promotion of tourism in Georgia has increased the demand for food, which, given the agricultural crisis, can only be met by increasing imports. Given the agflationary processes in the global economy, agflation is thus also being imported into Georgia. It is therefore hardly surprising that

40 percent of the population is living below the poverty line and 64 percent of the self-employed population has an income below the minimum subsistence level.

In its search for a model of economic development, Georgia has officially adopted a pro-European stance, but it has not taken any practical steps in this direction. A glaring example of this is the way the government behaved over the FTA with the EU. President Saakashvili has also publicly stated that Georgia should follow Singapore's model of economic development. By initiating its policy of Singaporization of the Georgian economy, the Saakashvili government is in fact increasingly distancing Georgia from the EU and generally from a European-style economic system.

Potential Scenarios and the Situation Most Likely to Be in Place by 2020

One scenario that can be ruled out in relation to Georgia's economic policy up to 2020 is the continued promotion of consumerism. The outcome of the parliamentary elections held on October 1, 2012, means that there is virtually no chance of this scenario unfolding, since the elections were won by the opposition coalition, Georgian Dream, headed by the billionaire Bidzina Ivanishvili. During its election campaign, Georgian Dream criticized the economic policy of the Saakashvili government and focused on the promotion of the real sector of the economy, along with social support for the poor segments of the population. Ivanishvili, now head of the

Becoming European

government that he himself formed, has begun to implement his preelection promises.

Based on these new realities, a more realistic scenario is the stepping up of negotiations with Brussels on an FTA with the EU. The new government's announcements that it will implement antimonopoly regulation and a European-style consumer rights protection system support this view. Antimonopoly regulation will help competition to develop. Together with an end to unofficial government intervention in business, signaled loudly and clearly on more than one occasion by the leaders of Georgian Dream, the demonopolizing of the Georgian economy will provide a significant impetus for business development.

It is entirely feasible that Georgia will achieve an FTA with the EU by 2014 at the latest. This would in itself attract private investment into Georgia's real sector of the economy, since the combination of a relatively low-cost (compared with the EU) workforce with a simplified system of business registration and relatively low tax burdens (again compared with the EU) could act as a stimulus for job creation in the Georgian economy. Given that the EU economy is currently 1,000 times the size of Georgia's economy, an FTA with the EU would massively expand the market for Georgian goods.

Once Georgia starts manufacturing high-quality products for the EU market, there will also be a demand for these products in the Turkish market in view of the FTA already reached with Turkey in 2008. This scenario for the development of the Georgian economy, based on reaching an FTA with the EU and a growth in exports to the EU and Turkey, appears entirely realistic.

Given that almost four years have passed since the signing of the charter between the United States and Georgia, without any negotiations on a free-trade regime even having started, the earliest expected date for an FTA with the United States is likely to be closer to 2020. This agreement, even if it is actually achieved, will therefore have little impact on the Georgian economy before 2020.

Resumption of full-scale trading relations with Russia is difficult to predict, since this is more of a political than an economic issue. The fact that Georgia and Russia are both members of the World Trade Organization (WTO) is not in itself a sufficient condition for establishing trade between the two countries. This means that it is virtually impossible to predict a resumption of trade with Russia in any forecast of Georgia's economic development up to 2020.

Achieving full-scale trading relations with Russia also raises the question of reopening the Trans-Caucasus Railway. The railway passes through Abkhazia, linking Georgia and Armenia with Russia, but was suspended back in August 1992.

Based on the realistic scenario whereby an FTA is reached with the EU, opening up trade with Turkey, the likely average economic growth in Georgia in the period 2013 to 2020 would be between 5 and 10 percent. The more pessimistic figure of 5 percent assumes that the global economic crisis will worsen; the more optimistic figure of 10 percent average growth assumes that the world economy will achieve steady growth.

However, this would mean that by 2020, Georgia's per capita GDP would be about 2.8 times the 2011 level, at USD 9,120 (in 2011, the figure was USD 3,215.4).

Studies on the comparative advantages of Georgia's economy have identified the main sectors as transportation, primarily of energy resources; agriculture and the food industry; hydroelectric power; and tourism. Clearly, the economic growth referred to earlier has to be provided by the sectors where Georgia has a comparative advantage. The government's emphasis on investing in the real sector of the economy means that industry's share of GDP would have to double on average by 2020, rising to at least 50 percent.

The natural and climatic conditions in Georgia also present enormous opportunities for developing agriculture, supported by an agriculture development fund currently being set up by the new government with an annual budget of GEL 1 billion (about USD 604 million as of January 14, 2013). This could increase agriculture's share of GDP to around 30 percent by 2020, which would be 3.5 times what it is now.

Developing the real economy, passing new European-style labor legislation, and a suitable social policy, taken together, will help to improve the quality of life of Georgia's citizens, which could lead to at least a 2.5 times reduction in poverty levels. On the basis of World Bank figures on global economic development, by 2020, Georgia's economic situation will be better than the current situation in EU countries such as Bulgaria and Romania, but worse than that in Latvia and Lithuania.

Vladimer Papava

Proposals and Recommendations

A primary objective for the Georgian government is to sign an FTA with the EU as quickly as possible in order to realize the full potential entailed in economic integration with the EU. To do this, the Georgian government needs to focus its economic policy on promoting production by implementing European models of antimonopoly regulation, consumer rights protection, and labor relations.

Negotiations on establishing a free-trade regime with the United States must be launched under the US Georgia Charter on Strategic Partnership. However, it is very important that the terms of an FTA with the United States do not conflict with the terms of an FTA with the EU. This requires coordination between Brussels and Washington, with the active engagement of Tbilisi in the process.

The new Georgian government must not stand in the way of Georgian companies wanting to return to the Russian market. These companies must themselves present the office of the chief public sanitary inspector of Russia with all necessary documentation confirming the quality of the products they manufacture, as well as evidence that these commodities are present in the markets of various countries of the world (the US, EU countries, China, Japan, etc.). If their products are once again banned from the Russian market, the Georgian government must defend these companies' interests under the WTO framework.

Implementing these recommendations will stimulate the expansion of Georgia's export potential, which is a priority for its socioeconomic development.

Topics for Discussion

The following topics can be singled out for discussion:

- How steady will the new Georgian government's focus be on developing the real sector of the economy by reaching an FTA with the EU? This is an important issue, given the system of dual power currently in place. Accordingly, the local offices of the state administration are subordinate not to the government but to President Saakashvili, who has officially declared that he is moving to the opposition.
- What positive impact can an FTA with the EU have on the Georgian economy if the eurozone crisis continues?
- How likely is an FTA with the United States by 2020, and how might this affect the Georgian economy?
- How likely is the resumption of normal trading relations with Russia? Even if this issue is resolved, will these trading relations reach the level at which they were when suspended in 2006?
- How would opening the railway passing through Abkhazia and linking Georgia and Armenia with the

southern regions of the Russian Federation affect the economy—both following the resumption of trading relations between Georgia and Russia and if the status quo is maintained?

The Georgian Model of Libertarianism and Its Applicability to Ukraine

September 29, 2014[*]

Ukraine has garnered the world's attention as a country facing a myriad of complex challenges, among which economic problems play a significant role. The corruption-stricken government of Ukraine is reminiscent of Georgia in the beginning of the twenty-first century, also in terms of the economy. Corruption is a key reason why neither the Georgian government in the fall of 2003 nor the Ukrainian government ten years later were able to quell the protest rallies.

---

[*] V. Papava, "The Georgian Model of Libertarianism and Its Applicability to Ukraine," *Democracy & Freedom Watch*, September 29, 2014, https://dfwatch.net/the-georgian-model-of-libertarianism-and-its-applicability-to-ukraine-53714-31393.

Given these similarities, let's consider the issue of whether it is suitable for Ukraine to take into account Georgia's experience with economic reforms. This issue has become more relevant after the Ukrainian government invited Georgia's former president, Mikheil Saakashvili, as an advisor, as well as Kakha Bendukidze, a former government member and one of the primary figures behind the Saakashvili government's economic reforms.

Foundations of the Georgian Model of Libertarianism

After the Rose Revolution in November 2003, Georgia began a series of reforms. In the spring of 2004, a Russian tycoon of Georgian origins, Kakha Bendukidze, was invited to work for the Georgian government. As director of the holding company Unified Machinery Plants ("Ob'yedinionnye mashostroitel'nye zavody"), he was quite closely connected to the Putin regime, which is not surprising if we take into account that the plants that comprised the holding company were building complex machinery, including equipment for producing atomic energy.

Mr. Bendukidze is famous for making libertarian statements that created a predisposition toward the economic reforms in Georgia that began in 2003. These reforms were referred to as libertarian at the international level. This opinion was supported by the fact that most of the licenses and permits necessary to start a business were abolished, and application rules were simplified for the remaining ones.

Becoming European

Furthermore, the system for issuing various types of documents by state agencies was significantly simplified, and the tax burden was eased. This made Georgia a leader in reforms, according to the World Bank's "Ease of Doing Business" ranking list. However, Georgia's economic growth was falling behind its neighboring country, Armenia, which was headed by a nonlibertarian government. Another of Georgia's other neighbors, Azerbaijan, experienced economic growth primarily through increased oil and gas extraction and exports. Thus, its economic growth is unsuitable for comparison. Specifically, according to World Bank data, Georgia and Armenia had nearly equal GDP per capita in 2002 and 2003, while in 2011 this indicator in Georgia was only 94 percent of Armenia's per capita GDP.

In parallel with these reforms, the Georgian government regularly violated property rights and did not shy away from making entrepreneurs wire some part of their profits to extrabudgetary funds. This certainly did not apply to the businesses closely associated with government members.

Also, the judicial system was directly under the control of the prosecutor's office, which was pointed out by a number of international and local observers. Unfortunately, the so-called libertarians in the government neither expressed any protest nor made any comments about these very unlibertarian aspects, and they may actually be better characterized as neo-Bolshevik in style.

As a rule, it is not surprising at all that human beings are libertarians for themselves, because they do not want others to interfere in their business or to restrict their rights in any way. A true libertarian is a person who is a libertarian for the sake of others, and as a result a libertarian in general.

A major peculiarity of the Georgian model of libertarianism created by Mr. Bendukidze is its key principle: "Libertarianism only for one's own business." Like their leader, most of the team members recruited by Mr. Bendukidze did not have an academic background in economics. Without knowing economics, it was easiest for them to share libertarian views; when one does not know about or understand market failures and the challenges of overcoming them, it is very easy to view a minimum of state interference as the only valid principle.

Thus, Georgian libertarians differ from true libertarians, because for Georgians, libertarianism was not a choice based on knowledge and understanding of economics. Quite the contrary—for them, it was a mask to cover an absence of economic knowledge.

Georgian Lessons of Pseudo-Libertarianism for Ukraine

In 2005, on the initiative of the Georgian libertarians, the Georgian antimonopoly law was abolished. When in the fall of 2007, President Saakashvili tasked the Ministry of Internal Affairs with creating antimonopoly regulation of monopolistic markets of salt and sugar, the pseudo-libertarians did not express any protest. They maintained their silence in 2006 when Russia banned the import of Georgian agricultural products and President Saakashvili tasked the defense minister with identifying potential international markets for Georgian wine. As a result, the Department of Wine Export was established within the Ministry of Defense. Unfortunately, there are more than a few similar examples.

In order to sign the Deep and Comprehensive Free Trade Agreement (DCFTA) with the EU, Georgia was required to meet the conditions imposed by Brussels: adoption of antimonopoly, food-safety, and labor laws. The Georgian libertarians delayed it for as long as they could. President Saakashvili's favorite appeal was the Singaporization of Georgia. Thus, it is not surprising that Georgia did not meet a major part of the EU requirements and sign the Association Agreement, which includes the DCFTA, in June 2014 after Saakashvili's National Movement and its leader were no longer in power.

The Georgian libertarians were not against the sale of vital national infrastructure to Russian state-owned companies; on the contrary, they facilitated it. The most illustrating example was the purchase of a controlling stake in a Georgian bank by the Russian state-owned bank VTB in 2005. Another example is the sale of two hydropower plants in Georgia to the Russian state-owned company Inter RAO. This happened after the Russia-Georgia war in 2008. The initiative by Georgian libertarians to sell a transiting gas pipeline (Russia-Armenia) built during the Communist period to Gazprom was prevented by the Americans in 2006.

It is doubtful that if Ukraine is truly eager to lead the country toward Euro-integration that such a pseudo-libertarian, or even a true libertarian, will be of any assistance, as the European market is clearly one based on state regulations. At the same time, it should be noted that Ukraine will benefit from the above-mentioned positive experience of Georgia in stimulating businesses.

As for combatting corruption, it primarily depends on the political will of the Ukrainian government. Georgia can serve as a strong example for Ukraine in this regard. The country's attacks on corruption, which began before the so-called pseudo-libertarian era that doubled tax revenues in the national budget over a very short period of time.

Finally, in order to receive relevant advice on conducting economic reforms, it is not necessary to reinvent the wheel. For this purpose, it is necessary to cooperate closely with the IMF and the World Bank, and most importantly, to share and utilize the recommendations from Brussels.

20

Economic Models of Eurasianism and the Eurasian Union: Why the Future is Not Optimistic

October 29, 2015[*]

A new Russia-Kazakhstan regional project named the Eurasian Economic Union (EAEU) was launched in 2015. Specifically, as of January 1, 2015, integrated economic processes among Belarus, Kazakhstan, and Russia are governed by the EAEU treaty. As of January 2, Armenia joined the EAEU, and as of May 21, Kyrgyzstan also became a member. In 2011, after the president of Russia declared the establishment of the Eurasian Union, some politicians and experts perceived it as a final victory of Eurasianism ideology in Russia. Under

---

[*] V. Papava, "Economic Models of Eurasianism and the Eurasian Union: Why the Future Is Not Optimistic," *The Central Asia-Caucasus Analyst*, October 29, 2015, http://cacianalyst.org/publications/analytical-articles/item/13296.

such circumstances, there is a need to analyze the economic models of Eurasianism and the Eurasian Union for a better understanding of their future.

Background

The goal of the Eurasianism Doctrine, which is one of the strongest Russian geopolitical schools formed in the 1920s, is to establish a special historical and cultural role for Russia in Eurasia. Public interest toward this theory increased in Russia, while its essential modernization took place in the 1990s when, after the collapse of the Soviet Union, Russia was seeking an imperial and integrating doctrine that would serve its purpose.

According to the economic model of Eurasianism, the market principle does not undermine ideocracy or the basis for ideological fundamentals to dominate public and political life. For Eurasianists, the market and private ownership belong to a pragmatically allowable and pragmatically useful realm, based on which, instead of a market economy, they recognize society with a market. Consequently, the objective of the Eurasianism economy is to maintain and develop all economic systems reflecting the cultural and historical path of the peoples living in the states of Eurasia.

Eurasianists prefer the principle of possession over the principle of ownership. In the first case, the proprietor is to abide by his social responsibilities and be oriented to the welfare goals of society, meaning that he is accountable to society and the state. Additionally, the state is to facilitate national production and carry out a paternalistic policy, applying mechanisms of tariff and nontariff protectionism in parallel. It is difficult to envisage how the economic model of Eurasianism can actually be implemented in a country given the modern processes of globalization ongoing worldwide.

According to Eurasianists, the Eurasian economic community, based on the above-discussed principles, will establish a so-called fourth zone that will essentially differ from other gigantic economic zones—such as America, Europe and the Pacific—but will also oppose them.

It is noteworthy that considering the characteristics of the economic model of Eurasianism (such as, for instance, society with the market, state ownership, and the guarantee to achieve the welfare goals of society), the economy of Belarus is the closest to these characteristics, considering the governance regime in the country, while in Armenia and Kazakhstan, especially, and at the beginning of the post-Soviet era in Kyrgyzstan and Russia as well, market reforms were carried out with more or less success.

The main goal of the EAEU at this stage is to deepen the trade and economic integration of its member countries, which is not even theoretically linked in any way with the economic model of Eurasianism. A key economic motif that facilitates the integration process is the existence of a redistributive mechanism of revenues from oil and gas. Specifically, within the EAEU no export duty is imposed, as a result of which the price of a given resource is reduced by the amount of the export duty as compared with that of the resource on the world market. Thus, the domestic production is indirectly subsidized. Export duties are collected when commodities leave the borders of the EAEU, resulting in the redistribution of some of the revenues to be received by Russia to the benefit of other member countries.

As oil and gas comprise a main export product for Russia, it is the redistribution of the revenues received from these commodities that is a key economic motive for integration. Although the scheme on which the EAEU is based is not economically profitable for Russia, it is a scheme that secures the gradual reanimation of the Soviet Union in its modernized form, which is the imperial ambition of Moscow.

Implications

Starting as early as 2011, Russia has been considering the possibility of concluding agreements on Free Economic Zones (FEZ) with certain countries (such as New Zealand, Vietnam, Israel, India, and the USA) and with regional unions (such as the ASEAN, EFTA, and EU). On May 29, 2015, such an agreement was signed with Vietnam, while negotiations with other countries and regional unions have been suspended or not even started, owing to political reasons.

According to the economic forecasts of Russian economists (they covered the three founding members of the EAEU, which are Belarus, Kazakhstan, and Russia), if FEZ agreements are concluded, both in the short and long terms, the EAEU as a whole, Russia, and Kazakhstan will benefit economically from these agreements, while Belarus will not benefit if the other party to a FEZ agreement is an economically developed country. Armenia and Kyrgyzstan are most likely to be in the same situation as Belarus. Considering that all members of the EAEU have veto power, in the case of the concluding of a FEZ agreement, in order to prevent Belarus (and any other member country in the same situation) from exercising its veto power, it is necessary to develop a redistribution mechanism benefiting Belarus and similar member countries.

As Russia annexed Crimea, and because of the armed conflict in Eastern Ukraine, the United States, which was subsequently joined by other countries, imposed economic sanctions against Russia as of the spring of 2014. This was a new challenge for the EAEU, as the sanctions do not apply to its other member states. As of August 2014, Moscow imposed so-called anti-sanctions, thereby anti-ing the existing sanctions against Russia and banning the import of food products from the USA, the EU, Australia, Norway, and Canada.

As the sanctions are only imposed against Russia and do not apply to other member counties of the EAEU, these countries have not joined the anti-sanctions as imposed by Russia. Therefore, the import of goods that were banned by Moscow in Russia may enter the territory of Russia from these EAEU member countries. This possibility is not excluded by the common customs territory of the EAEU, which includes all its member countries.

The now one-year experience of the anti-sanctions shows that it is Russia that incurs losses. It is straightforward that the existing situation absolutely opposes the principle of the common customs territory of the EAEU. In effect, this territory is divided into two areas: that of Russia and that of the other EAEU member countries.

The probability that the other member countries of the EAEU will voluntarily join Moscow in its anti-sanctions is low, since this would be economically unsuitable for these countries. If Moscow applies any mechanism to influence these countries, this will further undermine the already vulnerable foundations of the EAEU and raise questions about its future.

Additionally, it is notable that if Moscow should use any form of influence against the member countries, it will scare away others that are not yet members and that may be considered by Moscow in its plans as potential new members of the EAEU. Because of its political ambitions, it can be said that it is almost guaranteed that Moscow will not say no to anti-sanctions until the sanctions imposed against Russia are abolished. Thus, it is now less likely that the existing system of sanctions and anti-sanctions will be changed at the expense of any compromise made by Moscow.

Conclusion

It can be stated that it is utopian that the economic model of Eurasianism can be realized in the modern global world, while the economic model of the EAEU is not only unstable but also inadequate. This has become most apparent as a result of the sanctions imposed against Russia and the anti-sanctions introduced by Moscow.

21

For Georgia, GEENTRANCE is Coming!

January 5, 2017[*]

In October 2016, a post-Soviet Georgia successfully passed yet another exam in democratic development. As international observers recognized, the parliamentary elections were conducted in a competitive, fair, and mostly peaceful environment. Georgia, a small country in the Caucasus, stands out among other post-Soviet countries: following the Baltic nations, Georgia is the most successful country in building democratic institutions, strengthening the market economy, and developing steps toward Euro-Atlantic integration.

Take, for example, the country's intensive cooperation with NATO within the framework of the Partnership for

---

[*] V. Papava, "For Georgia GEENTRANCE Is Coming!" *Eurasia Review*, January 5, 2017, https://www.eurasiareview.com/05012017-for-georgia-geentrance-is-coming-oped/.

Peace project. At the NATO summit in Prague in 2002, the then-president of Georgia, Eduard Shevardnadze, officially declared that Georgia is committed to becoming a NATO member country. Since 2001, Georgian military officers have continuously been participating in NATO military operations.

Despite the fact that Georgia gains the highest praise from NATO leaders for its efforts in this regard, getting the much-desired Membership Action Plan (MAP), not to mention full NATO membership itself, remains unattainable for Georgia. Georgians have often heard from Brussels in recent years that NATO's door is open to Georgia, but no open door is useful if you are unable to pass through. Georgians do know that Russia cannot directly veto a NATO decision because Russia is not a NATO member, but they also realize that Russia has a huge impact on some of the Western European countries that are blocking Georgia's access to the alliance.

Soon, it will be a quarter-century that Georgia has been cooperating with the European Union, but this Caucasian country attained its greatest achievement in June 2014 when the EU-Georgia Association Agreement was signed. As of July 1, 2016, as well, we have the coming into force of the Deep and Comprehensive Free Trade Area (DCFTA). It is also to be highlighted that Georgia met all the preconditions for obtaining EU visa liberalization, but due to the large influx of immigrants into the bloc, Brussels is not in a hurry to deliver on the obligation it undertook in terms of easing EU travel.

There are obvious obstacles on the road to NATO and the EU; however, these are caused not so much by Georgia

Becoming European

but by the alliance and the union themselves. This raises some skepticism. A political party of a non-Western orientation was just elected to the parliament of Georgia in the October elections and will be represented with a small faction. This is perhaps the first red flag that Georgians are losing hope, not to mention trust, in the West, NATO, and the EU.

Among the supporters of Georgia's independent statehood, the United States is the most robust proponent among all the Western countries—although it can be said that this support has not been as strong from President Barack Obama's administration as it was from his predecessors. However, the United States still remains Georgia's strongest strategic partner, and so Tbilisi is watching President Trump's upcoming administration with great expectations.

One-fifth of Georgia's territory is illegally occupied by Russia, which continues to carry out its creeping annexation of the country. Under these circumstances, the Western-oriented Georgia needs not just general statements of support but truly effective actions. The example of Cyprus is worth noting, as its northern part is under Turkish occupation and not controlled by the capital, Nicosia. This sets a positive precedent for Georgia in that the country, despite the Russian occupation, may still one day be integrated into the EU.

Russia's most recent project is the Eurasian Economic Union (EAEU), which consists of four countries (Armenia, Belarus, Kazakhstan, and Kyrgyzstan) under the umbrella of Russia. Two of these EAEU countries border Georgia in the north (Russia) and the south (Armenia). Georgia's position in the middle of this Eurasian sandwich means that providing effective support for its Western orientation is of key importance.

Although Georgia still has a long way to go to be in line and harmonized with EU standards, it may also be credited as being far away from the trends in the EAEU. For instance, according to the Corruption Perceptions Index study conducted by Transparency International, the most corrupt country in the EU in 2015 was Bulgaria (it ranks in 69th place among the least corrupt countries worldwide). Armenia is the least corrupt country in the EAEU, while it ranks in 95th place worldwide. The most corrupt countries in the EAEU are Kazakhstan and Kyrgyzstan, which share 123rd place worldwide. For comparison, Georgia ranks in 48th place, and this shows that it is definitely closer to European standards (of the most recent EU members, Latvia ranks in 40th place and Croatia, Hungary, and Slovakia in 50th). It is not surprising that Georgia does not want to return to its corrupt past.

We consider that becoming an EU member country is not a goal but a means that will allow the Georgian population to live in a dignified European style. Everyone knows that the EU has to tackle a range of drastic problems in its own backyard: immigration, the Eurozone crises, and now Brexit. Georgia understands the EU's difficulties, as well as NATO's cautionary approach toward Russia. But it is incomprehensible that Tbilisi meets its obligations undertaken before the EU and NATO yet is taken no further than the simple expressed recognition of Georgia's achievements on its road toward Western approximation and integration.

This is a point in history when the West needs to recognize that there is a small country in the Caucasus, perhaps one of the most strategic regions in the world, that is pursuing democratic values but encounters obstacles on its way to truly becoming a part of the Western family of nations. GEENTRANCE means that Georgia's entrance has started and its integration process with the West is being implemented with more or less success. It is crucial now that the West believe that GEENTRANCE is underway. GEENTRANCE is coming!

22

Post-Communist Georgia Between Two Alternatives: EU and the EAEU

February 1, 2017[*]

Georgia today stands at a crossroads between two alternatives: to continue rapprochement with the European Union (EU) on a basis of the Association Agreement (and to ultimately pursue membership through a lengthy, drawn-out process) or to join the Eurasian Economic Union (EAEU), a much simpler prospect. Georgia has long made clear that it favors engagement with Europe and Euro-Atlantic institutions; however, discussion of Georgia's rapprochement with Russia

---

[*] V. Papava, "Post-Communist Georgia Between Two Alternatives: EU and the EAEU," *The Post-Soviet Post, CSIS—Center for Strategic & International Studies*, February 1, 2017, https://www.csis.org/blogs/post-soviet-post/guest-post-post-communist-georgia-between-two-alternatives-eu-and-eaeu.

Becoming European

is becoming more and more topical as a result of uncertainty in modern Georgia-Russia relations and the establishment of the EEAU. This essay clarifies the main differences between the EU and EAEU in the wider context of Georgia's future.

The EAEU started operations in 2015 and at present includes five member-countries: Armenia, Belarus, Kazakhstan, Kyrgyzstan, and Russia. Georgia is located between two member states—Armenia and Russia—which creates new challenges for Georgia's development. Georgia and the EU signed the EU-Georgia Association Agreement in June 2014. Despite this agreement, talks on Georgia's rapprochement with Russia have recently reignited, largely sparked by the establishment of the EAEU.

When analyzing the suitability of these two organization for Georgia, it is important to consider the essential differences between them:

- The EU was initially set up as an economic union, with the aim of promoting the economic development of its member states. Although the EAEU contains the term *economic* in its title, this union is not so much a means of economic development as it is a mechanism through which Moscow seeks to maintain and increase its political influence on the member states.
- The EU is, with the partial exception of some Eastern European member states, an association of developed economies, while the EAEU is comprised solely of underdeveloped post-Soviet economies deficient in

their market institutions and lagging behind global standards in technology.

- Transparency International's Corruption Perceptions Index demonstrates an essential disparity between the EU and EAEU on the issue of corruption. The most corrupt state in the EU, according to this ranking, is Bulgaria (75th of 175), while the least corrupt in the EAEU is Belarus (79th). For comparison, Georgia ranks 44th.

- For a country to join the EU, it must meet certain standards set by Brussels in areas such as democratic institutions, human rights, freedom of speech and expression, and market economy. Furthermore, only after an applicant country has met European standards in the above areas is the issue of formal membership placed on the agenda. In order to encourage rapprochement with the EU, Brussels has adopted special formats of cooperation: for instance, the European Neighborhood Policy (ENP) instrument and the Eastern Partnership (EaP). Georgia is a participant in both formats. It is through the application of the EaP framework that Georgia has managed to successfully traverse the rather difficult path toward the entry into force of the Deep and Comprehensive Free Trade Area (DCFTA) and the Association Agreement. Unlike the EU, the EAEU has virtually no complex preconditions for membership. On the contrary, Moscow's aim is to expand the union in order to increase its political influence on member states via economic leverage, with no concern for economic and political standards like those emphasized by the EU.

When the essential differences between the EU and the EAEU are summed up, it can be concluded that Georgia can more easily attain membership in the latter than in the former. However, this evokes a separate question: why would Georgia, a country with a more or less EU-level standard of corruption, enter into the much more corrupt EAEU, which lags behind the EU in institutional and technological terms and serves Moscow's political objective of strengthening Russian control over the member states? The answer, of course, is that it would not be in Georgia's interest to pursue EAEU membership.

Moreover, it is important to emphasize that the commensurability barrier for the EAEU is much more significant than for the EU. Ruslan Greenberg, a Russian economist, outlines this issue through the comparison of the Commonwealth of Independent States (CIS) and the EU. Greenberg shows that an alliance of countries is streamlined and possesses a higher chance of success when the commensurables (sizes) of the member countries are more or less comparable.

When an alliance of countries is formed, the states concerned should make a decision on the areas where they are ready to relinquish part of their sovereignty in favor of the supranational governing bodies of the association. When the commensurability of the countries is more or less analogous, reaching consensus on this matter is easier than when one country and its economy are several times larger in size than those of all the other constituents of the union put together. In this case, the largest country finds it difficult to imagine how it can be expected to yield a share of its sovereignty equivalent to that of much smaller states. As a result, this large country attempts to relinquish far less of its state sovereignty than it obligates the other smaller member states to surrender, thereby maintaining a dominant position in the association.

One of the reasons for the EU's success is that it consolidates relatively large and simultaneously commensurably more or less homogeneous countries, such as Germany, Great Britain (before the implementation of Brexit), Italy, and France, and relatively small but commensurably comparable countries, such as Belgium, Ireland, and the Netherlands.

According to Greenberg, the commensurability barrier for the CIS was rather high, since the Russian economy accounted for 67–70 percent of the entire economy of the CIS. This barrier is even larger in the EAEU, as Russia's constitutes over 82 percent of the entire economy of the union. The issue of the commensurability barrier is a further indication that the EAEU does not have a high chance of success, and an additional factor to give Georgian policymakers pause when considering membership in this union.

23

Georgia's Modern Decisions and Threats of Expansion of Russian Presence in Caucasus

February 26, 2017[*]

Soon after the 2016 parliamentary elections, the government of the party of the Georgian Dream (GD), which won the elections, started discussions and implemented some actions, both of which create new threats for the country's economic and energy independence.

---

[*] V. Papava, "Georgia's Modern Decisions and Threats of Expansion of Russian Presence in Caucasus," *Eurasia Review*, February 26, 2017, https://www.eurasiareview.com/26022017-georgias-modern-decisions-and-threats-of-expansion-of-russian-presence-in-caucasus-oped/.

Vladimer Papava

Sale of Georgia's Strategic Assets

To build trust within the parliament, in his address, Prime Minister Giorgi Kvirikashvili stated that the government would consider the initial public offering (IPO) of 25 percent of the state-owned Georgian Railway and the Georgian Oil and Gas Corporation stakes.

The disposal of Georgia's strategic assets is in no way a novel concept, as the United National Movement (UNM) government, in power 2003–2012, did not recognize the existence of such assets and considered that selling them to Russia harbored no security threats for Georgia. All the more, this took place in light of Moscow's public announcement of its intention to establish a "liberal empire" (Torbakov 2003)—in other words, secure influence over the post-Soviet space and beyond by applying economic mechanisms (Papava and Starr 2006).

Given that gas pipelines and railways in Armenia are owned by Russian state companies (gas pipelines are owned by Gazprom, while the railway is administered by Russian Railways, a company that went so far as to rename the state-owned Armenian Railways the South Caucasus Railways in an overt acknowledgement of Moscow's intention to establish control over the Georgian and, ultimately, Azerbaijani railways), it is evident that if even 25 percent of the Georgian Railway and Georgian Oil and Gas Corporation shares are put up for sale, Russian companies will be the primary stakeholders.

Due to the Armenian-Azerbaijani conflict, Azerbaijani companies may also emerge as buyers of Georgian assets as Baku seeks to acquire new economic mechanisms to exert pressure on Yerevan. In this case, Tbilisi will certainly be embroiled in the Armenia-Azerbaijan confrontation, which is definitely not within Georgia's interests. It is unfortunate that the GD continues to pursue the same policies threatening Georgian national interests as the UNM government had throughout the nine years of its tenure.

Russian Gas Transit Fees to Armenia

Already, during Eduard Shevardnadze's presidency, Tbilisi and Moscow had signed an agreement that authorized Georgia to retain, as a transit fee, 10 percent of the gas transported by Gazprom via the pipeline through Georgia into Armenia. In January 2016, Gazprom initiated talks with the Georgian Ministry of Energy seeking to replace the transit-fee disbursement in the form of natural gas with cash amounting to 10 percent of the value of the transported commodity.

Gazprom's proposition is undoubtedly economically unprofitable for Georgia. We should recall that in 2006, Gazprom announced that as of 2007, it would supply gas to both Georgia and Armenia at higher rates: USD 230 per 1,000 m3 instead of USD 110. Moreover, Gazprom would agree to uphold the previous tariff provided it gained ownership of gas distribution facilities, the cumulative value of which would be equal to the difference between the new and old tariffs multiplied by the amount of gas consumed. Unlike Georgia, Armenia agreed to this proposition, effectively transferring ownership of its gas distribution systems to Gazprom.

Subsequently, against the background of Armenia's rapprochement with Russia, the price of gas supplied by Gazprom to Armenia experienced a decline. It is evident that due to the price differences, Georgia will be unable to purchase the same amount of gas with the monetized payment that it would have received in the form of natural gas for supporting transit to Armenia.

The impression that the Georgian government would concede to Gazprom's amendments to the payment method for gas transit fees was followed by sharply critical assessments and protest rallies. As a result, the Minister of Energy managed to reach an agreement with Gazprom according to which existing transit terms—namely, the commodity-based payment scheme—would be retained throughout 2016 (for one year).

By 2017, talks between Gazprom and the Ministry of Energy on the gas transit fee payment method resumed, and unfortunately, the energy minister agreed to Gazprom's proposal. Perhaps the Georgian government managed to preserve the transit fee payment terms in 2016 on account of Tbilisi's explanation to Moscow that due to the upcoming parliamentary elections, it would have been highly unlucrative for the incumbent GD government and parliamentary majority to introduce amendments to gas transit terms. Thus, a one-year postponement was requested.

Becoming European

It is noteworthy that already in November 2016, Armenia announced that the price of gas for local consumers would decrease as, starting in 2017, Gazprom would reduce gas transit fees for Georgia by monetizing the commodity payments (NGW 2016). Evidently, this information (the fact that Gazprom expected concessions on Tbilisi's part in terms of amendments to the transit fee payment method and reductions in the amount of gas thus available to Georgia whereby Yerevan made its assurances regarding consumer tariff cuts) should have been available to the Georgian government. If the Georgian side was still obliged to cut transit fees, it would have been more prudent to retain the commodity payment scheme and agree to a smaller share instead of the 10 percent of transported gas.

It is imperative to consider that Georgia is located between two member states of the newly established Eurasian Economic Union (EAEU); thus, the threat that Georgia will be compelled to join the union is substantial. Moreover, this time, Tbilisi has handed over its energy leverage to Moscow, since Gazprom can now also make concessions by allowing Georgia to purchase 10 percent of the gas transported to Armenia (previously retained as transit payment) using the cash obtained as the current transit fee if Georgia becomes an EAEU member. It should be emphasized that the economic basis for the existence of the EAEU is underpinned by the redistribution mechanism for revenues generated by energy resources.

Georgian MPs have assessed this harmful decision as "optimal" and "maximal." They have attributed the economic losses resulting from their weakness (at best) to the "market principle."

Conclusion

The main root cause for Georgia's modern government taking such steps at best lies in unprofessionalism and a denial of universally recognized knowledge of economics, contemporary geopolitics, and geoeconomics.

References

NGW. 2016. "Armenia Cuts Gas Price Again." *Natural Gas World*, November 7, https://www.naturalgasworld.com/armenia-cuts-gas-price-again-34312 (last accessed February 21, 2017).

Papava, V., and F. Starr. 2006. "Russia's Economic Imperialism." *Project Syndicate*, January 17, https://www.project-syndicate.org/commentary/russia-s-economic-imperialism?barrier=accesspaylog (last accessed February 21, 2017).

Torbakov, I. 2003. "Russian Policymakers Air Notion of "Liberal Empire" in Caucasus, Central Asia." *Eurasianet*, October 27, http://www.eurasianet.org/departments/insight/articles/eav102703.shtml (last accessed February 21, 2017).

24

Primitivism as a Trait of Georgia's Modern Economic Policy

May 4, 2017[*]

During the 2012 and 2016 electoral periods, the ruling Georgian Dream (GD) issued numerous pledges to voters, including economic guarantees that garnered special attention but nevertheless could not be implemented for several reasons. The GD government's economic policy has sustained some successes but also reflects features of economic primitivism—simplistic and populist economic policies—that risk hampering the evolution of Georgia's economy from a consumerist to an innovation economy.

---

[*] V. Papava, "Primitivism as a Trait of Georgia's Modern Economic Policy," *Central Asia-Caucasus Analyst*, May 4, 2017, http://cacianalyst.org/publications/analytical-articles/item/13444-primitivism-as-a-trait-of-georgia%E2%80%99s-modern-economic-policy.html.

Vladimer Papava

Background

The GD government managed to secure Georgia's signature on an Association Agreement (AA) with the EU in June 2014, entering into force on July 1, 2016. The AA and its introduction of a Deep and Comprehensive Free Trade Area (DCFTA) agreement with the EU should be assessed as the most significant accomplishments of the GD government.

An example of the GD government's optimistic economic vision is the approval in 2014 of the "Social-Economic Development Strategy of Georgia—Georgia 2020." According to the strategy, the Georgian government's economic policy should be based on three key principles:

1. Ensuring rapid and efficient economic growth driven by the development of the real sector of the economy
2. Implementation of economic policies that facilitate inclusive economic growth
3. Rational use of natural resources, the provision of environmental safety and sustainability, and natural-disaster risk mitigation throughout the process of economic development

The Georgian government has also instructed ministries and other state agencies to draw up midterm action plans based on Georgia 2020 by June 30 of every year. Unfortunately, the government has yet to fulfill this task, which has raised questions about the feasibility of the objectives and goals set forth in the strategy.

An important reason for this is the primitivism present in the GD government's economic thinking. The "Governmental 4-Point Plan" initiated by Prime Minister Giorgi Kvirikashvili was first introduced to businesspersons in early 2016. At the time, however, the plan itself did not exist in written form. The document outlining the four-point plan first appeared toward the end of GD's preelection program, "Freedom, Rapid Development, Well-Being," developed for the 2016 parliamentary elections. Subsequently, the plan was incorporated into the winning party's government program of the same name.

Implications

The four points of the plan are:

1. economic reform
2. education reform
3. spatial planning
4. governance reform.

However, the plan promotes the maintenance and reinforcement of a nonproductive and, at the same time, consumerist economic model in Georgia. Unfortunately, due to the low level of development of the real sector of the economy, the country consumes more than it produces. As a result, over the years, import is three to four times higher than export, while import goods constitute an average of 80 percent of the consumer basket (as well as the food basket).

The cornerstone of point 1 is the exemption of businesses from corporate income tax on reinvested profits. Under these circumstances, the plan will bolster those Georgian firms that are typical of a nonproductive and simultaneously consumerist economy. The system is known as the Estonian model and entered into force in Georgia in 2017. It is unclear why tax breaks for profit reinvestment should be granted to restaurants and hotels, not to mention the financial sector. Such businesses are abundant in the Georgian economy even without tax benefits. It would have been more advisable to afford tax breaks only to those firms within the real sector of the economy that apply innovative technology to reinvest their profit. Given the severe shortage of such firms, the Estonian model for corporate income tax will contribute to enhancing the consumerist structure of Georgia's economy, offering no incentives to the nearly nonexistent innovative real sector.

According to point 2, the vocational education system should be oriented toward a dual or work-based learning approach that entails training programs implemented jointly by educational institutions and potential employers. University education would be focused on the actual requirements of the economy, identified through labor market analysis. Yet once again, considering that Georgia has virtually no real sector or innovation economy, focusing the vocational education system solely on work-based learning approaches and university education solely on the actual requirements of the economy will not ensure the training of specialists befitting a knowledge-based economy. Thus, the focus of vocational and university education on current rather than prospective needs of the economy will further contribute to enhancing the consumerist structure of Georgia's economy.

Point 3 postulates that spatial planning measures around the country should be conducive to sustainable urban and rural development and the advancement of an inter-regional transport network, ultimately aiming to transform Georgia into a year-round tourist destination. It is noteworthy that tourism was a priority under both the United National Movement (UNM) and the GD governments. Given that 80 percent of Georgia's consumer and food baskets consist of import goods, the needs of tourists, as additional consumers, must be supplemented by additional import since Georgia produces only 20 percent of its food products and, unfortunately, none of the means of transportation or fuel necessary for travel within the country. Hence, the government tending solely to the development of tourism fails to contribute to the country's diverse economic development and sustains trends applicable to a consumerist economy.

Evidently, the first three points of the four-point plan contradict the country's innovative development strategy and therefore also Georgia 2020. Indeed, it unfortunately constitutes a vivid example of economic primitivism resulting from a disregard for economics. Since revenue otherwise generated from corporate income tax will now be deducted from the national budget, the government has called for increasing excise taxes and taxes on gambling. While increased taxes on gambling are seen as a positive development by both economists and society as a whole, the excise tax (on fuel and tobacco products) is projected to at least double, which raises serious doubts. First, this could at least partially drive the tobacco business into the shadow economy. Second, fuel price hikes will have a negative impact on the economy as a whole as well as on the social conditions of the population.

These measures raises questions as to why the reduction in tax revenues ensuing from the application of the Estonian model are compensated for only by raising excise taxes and why the government has not introduced other forms of taxation. During the UNM's tenure, Georgia's constitution was amended to state that the levying of any new taxes and all tax increases, aside from excise tax, can take place only via referendum. Regulating tax policy via referenda is clearly unjustified and devoid of any reason in this context; it can be said with confidence that the absolute majority of voters would oppose any tax increases or the imposition of any new taxes. Unfortunately, the GD government and parliamentary majority, which have resolved to revise the constitution, do not yet aim to conduct a referendum on tax policy or abolish these regulations.

Provided that the excise tax hike is an unpopular move, the government assumed an obligation to reduce budget expenditures in the national budget for 2017. Wage funds in the majority of budgetary organizations will decrease by 10 percent, and administrative costs will be reduced by the same share. The government also associates this step with point 4 of the plan, which aims to enhance governance efficiency. Regrettably, the government does not have a clear understanding of what "enhancing governance efficiency" entails. In this context, the 10 percent reduction of state administration constitutes a simplistic approach, as downsizing the government does not guarantee an increase in efficiency.

It is unfortunate that the government also fails to take into account that fuel price hikes or curtailing budgetary organizations under conditions of stimulated inflation will further complicate the social situation in the country and should not be in the government's political interests.

Conclusions

In the early stages of its tenure, the GD government took a number of steps associated with economic optimism. The signature of the AA with the EU is of historical significance, aligning Georgia's economy with the EU's DCFTA. In this context, the adoption of the Georgia 2020 strategy was essential, consolidating the government's aspiration to establish an innovation- and knowledge-based economy. Unfortunately, instead of tasking the ministries with developing action plans on the basis of a Georgia 2020 strategy (as envisioned by the government decree), the prime minister has entirely overlooked this complex document and replaced it with a primitive four-point plan whose implementation cannot and will not lead to the improvement of Georgia's distorted consumerist economic model.

The source of Georgian economic primitivism lies in unprofessionalism and the denial of universally recognized economic principles. Under these circumstances, international financial institutions and civil society have a particular role to play, since their engagement is virtually the only mechanism capable of exerting relatively effective pressure in order to eliminate economic primitivism and the replacement of incompetent personnel in the government.

25

Features of Governmental "Business" in Post-Soviet Georgia

June 27, 2017[*]

One of the most arguable issues among economists is how and to what extent the government should intervene in the economy. As we know, different economic theories give different recommendations, starting from nonintervention policy and finishing with the command economy structure. So, theoretically and practically, the range of governmental intervention in the economy is very broad. Nevertheless, most economists agree that the government should not have its own business or at least it should be primarily based on the idea of national security.

---

[*] V. Papava, "Features of Governmental 'Business' in Post-Soviet Georgia," *Eurasia Review*, June 27, 2017, https://www.eurasiareview.com/27062017-features-of-governmental-business-in-post-soviet-georgia-oped/.

In modern Georgia, a distinctive feature of governmental "business" is the sale of buildings held by ministries and other governmental institutions. The reason for this kind of privatization is not hidden in profit-making or any other economic benefits. The main reason for such business is traditionally called tourism development, placing hotels in former government buildings. Such an economic policy can hardly be evaluated as rational. It has obvious shades of primitivism.

One of the most prominent examples of the primitivistic approach of Georgian Dream (GD), the ruling political party, toward the economy can be seen in the privatization of the building of the Ministry of Economy in 2015. On the initiative of Prime Minister Giorgi Kvirikashvili, who was the acting Minister of Economy at that time, this building was purchased by a Chinese company, Hualing, on electronic auction for USD 9.45 million with the purpose of opening a hotel therein.

It is noteworthy that after the privatization, the Ministry of Economy decided to stay in the same building and paid rent to Hualling until a fire damaged the building. Because of the fire, the ministry paid a fine to the Chinese company, vacated the building, and rented new premises.

The sale of administrative buildings for the purpose of establishing hotels was initiated by the former government of the United National Movement (UNM). In particular, in 2007, buildings of the Ministry of Agriculture and the Ministry of Justice were used for the same purpose.

Becoming European

The main difference between the plans to convert ministry buildings into hotels under the UNM and the GD is as follows: for the UNM government, before starting a project of converting old buildings into hotels, the issue of moving a ministry to another building was solved (the Ministry of Agriculture was moved in to another state-owned building and the Ministry of Justice was moved to a brand new building that was built especially for this reason); meanwhile, the GD government sold the building of the Ministry of Economy but had no idea where to move the whole body.

Another interesting story happened in 2009 with the Ministry of Foreign Affairs when the UNM government decided to move the ministry (which had an emergency building) into a state-owned building in Tbilisi city center. GEL 10 million was spent on renovations to this building, but then the government suddenly changed its mind, and privatization was decided on instead for the purpose of opening a new hotel. This idea was successfully accomplished during the GD ruling period. In the summer of 2016, the Biltmore Tbilisi, a luxury hotel, was opened in this building, while the Ministry of Foreign Affairs is still in a temporary location.

In 2012, the UNM government moved the Parliament of Georgia from the capital city to Kutaisi (to support Kutaisi's economic development). The project cost the government GEL 350 million. The nonfunctional building of the Parliament in Tbilisi was aimed for privatization with the opening of a business center, hotels, and restaurants inside. Fortunately, after the 2012 elections, the GD government came to power, stopped the process of privatization, and returned the Tbilisi parliament building to its original function, together with the Kutaisi parliament building.

Given the saving the Tbilisi parliament building from privatization, it is even more difficult to understand the obviously pointless privatization of the Ministry of Economy by the GD government. In March 2017, the GD government took the initiative and announced the construction of a governmental city in one of the historic districts of Tbilisi where several ministries will be placed. While the Ministry of Economy is left without its own building, the Ministry of Foreign Affairs is located in an emergency building, and the building of the Ministry of Education and Science is in poor condition, the government's decision to build a governmental city in Tbilisi could be understood. However, it is obvious that neither the UNM nor the GD ever bothered to conduct a cost-benefit analysis for their strange business.

Unfortunately, the results of these dubious businesses are not important for the government. This is no longer even a business!

Belt and Road Initiative, the Russian Factor, and Main Challenges for Georgia

November 27, 2017[*]

Beijing's new global Belt and Road Initiative (BRI) includes the Silk Road Economic Belt and the 21st Century Maritime Silk Road. The Silk Road Economic Belt (SREB) is based on different economic corridors. One among these corridors, the Central Asia–West Asia Economic Corridor, is very important for Caucasian Georgia, which is located on it.

Georgia, together with its neighbor and strategic ally, Azerbaijan, has been considered in the context of the historical Great Silk Road right from the beginning of the 1990s. The

---

[*] V. Papava, "Belt and Road Initiative, the Russian Factor, and Main Challenges for Georgia," *Eurasia Review*, November 27, 2017, https://www.eurasiareview.com/27112017-belt-and-road-initiative-the-russian-factor-and-main-challenges-for-georgia-oped/.

practical implications of this idea have been the TRACECA project initiated by the EU in 1993 and the INOGATE project starting in 1996. In fact, practically all projects envisaged in terms of the Silk Road transport corridor are functioning successfully today.

The inclusion of Georgia (and Azerbaijan) in the SREB project is facilitated by the already implemented Silk Road Transport Corridor (SRTC) project. If we compare the SRTC or TRACECA and the SREB's Central Asia–West Asia Economic Corridor projects, the differences lie in at least two areas: the first project was initiated by the West (more specifically, the EU) while the second originated in China; and the first project is clearly and primarily a transport project while the second is much more complex, as it is economic.

According to the assessments of most analysts, one of the main threats to the successful functioning of the BRI (more specifically, the Central Asia–West Asia Economic Corridor) crossing Georgia and Azerbaijan is Russia. Moscow wants to not only retain but also expand its influence in the post-Soviet area. This is exactly why, from the very beginning, Moscow was not interested in the development of the SRTC crossing Azerbaijan and Georgia independently from Russia.

In order to balance the BRI initiative, Moscow put forward a Greater Eurasian Partnership (GEP) initiative, which is a large-scale vision of the Russian-Kazakh initiative started in 2015, the Eurasian Economic Union (EAEU). It aims at encompassing Russia, China, India, Iran, Turkey, and other countries, confronting US hegemony and Atlanticism in

Becoming European

general. At first glance, the GEP has formally similar scopes, objectives, and priorities as the OBOR initiative; however, for the government of the Russian Federation, the GEP is not just a large-scale economic cooperation project. Rather, it has quite a large geopolitical significance as well.

It is also noteworthy that the leadership of Russia and China signed a joint statement (PoR 2015) about cooperation between the EAEU and the SREB in May 2015 while reaffirming their statement about a solid partnership and cooperation between the EAEU and the OBOR initiative in June 2016 (PoR 2016). Despite this, it has still not been possible to sign agreements on future trade and economic cooperation between China and the EAEU.

The main reason can be identified as this: the Russian model of economic modernization, which relies mostly on the principles of consumer economics, has turned out to be utterly useless in comparison to the Chinese model, which is based upon the prioritization of innovation development. This is exactly why Russia significantly lags behind China in terms of economic and technological development, creating impediments for Moscow in establishing more or less equality-based economic relations with Beijing. According to the views of some experts, China's economic cooperation with the Central Asian countries and the membership of Kazakhstan and Kyrgyzstan in the Moscow-created EAEU, as well as a clear geopolitical approximation between Russia and China in recent years (especially in the energy sector), creates the probability that the EAEU and the SREB could move to a potential cooperation.

For developing the importance of the BRI initiative in Beijing's relations with Moscow, it could be instrumental for China to refuse to implement the paradigms of the predominant and confrontational alternative economic corridors. Instead of this, it would be more beneficial to move to the paradigm of the compatibility of economic corridors that would facilitate the harmonization of these corridors and their harmonic development. This is exactly why the GEC and BRI initiatives must be seen as complementary to one another.

Given the increased risk of terrorism and other industrial disasters in the contemporary world, it is important to have complementary transport and energy corridors that should ensure the maximum continuity of transport flows. The fact that the institution of a free trade regime between China and the EU is under active discussion is very important for Georgia. In this regard, the SREB creates a new stage in the economic cooperation between China and the EU.

China and Georgia are members of the World Trade Organization. The fact that a free trade agreement has been signed between the two countries is very important in terms of the development of trade relations. Georgia also has the Deep and Comprehensive Free Trade Area (DCFTA) agreement with the EU, as well as a free trade agreement with the European Free Trade Association (EFTA). Hence, the expansion of trade between the EU and China will enable Georgia to become a logistical hub connecting China with Europe—for which the Baku-Tbilisi-Kars railway and the implementation of the Anaklia Black Sea Deep Water Port project will have vital importance.

Of further note is that due to the transportation of Caspian oil and gas to Turkey, Georgia already plays the role of an energy resources transportation hub. For Georgia, the SREB project creates an opportunity to transform its role as an energy resources transportation hub to a regional economic hub in general.

In this regard, it should be underlined that with the DCFTA agreement signed between the EU and Georgia, products exported from Georgia to the EU must be produced in Georgia. This, therefore, makes Georgia attractive to all countries without free trade agreements with the EU to invest in Georgia and export the production manufactured here to the EU market. This includes China as well, which is already investing in Georgia. Consequently, Georgia can actually become an economic hub in the region, which would be in full accordance with the content of the Central Asia–West Asia Economic Corridor project crossing Georgia.

References

PoR. 2015. "Press Statements Following Russian-Chinese Talks." *President of Russia*, May 8, http://en.kremlin.ru/events/president/transcripts/49433 (last accessed November 20, 2017).

PoR. 2016. "Press Statements Following Russian-Chinese Talks." *President of Russia*, June 25, http://en.kremlin.ru/events/president/transcripts/52273 (last accessed November 20, 2017).

27

Georgia's Economy in a Tourist Trap

July 25, 2018[*]

For contemporary Georgia, economic development based upon inclusive economic growth has special importance. In the recent period, Georgia has experienced a high economic growth rate. Specifically, in May 2018, its real GDP growth was 7.5 percent as compared to the same period of 2017, while the average real growth in the first five months of 2018 was 6.1 percent.

Despite this, there is clear public discontent with the existing economic and social difficulties. More specifically, according to the data of the World Bank, one in two people in Georgian regions lives in extreme poverty, while Tbilisi enjoys a relatively better situation in this regard, with only one in five

---

[*] V. Papava, "Georgia's Economy in a 'Tourist Trap,'" *Rondeli Blog*, July 25, 2018, https://www.gfsis.org/blog/view/854.

people on the brink of starvation. According to UNICEF, one in five children in Georgia lives under the poverty line and one in six consumes less than the subsistence minimum. At the same time, about 33.4 percent of families with three or more children and 24.1 percent of families with one or two children were living in absolute poverty in 2017.

A logical question arises: if the country has a high economic growth rate, then why the public dissatisfaction? Could this be caused by Georgia's economy developing in the wrong direction? In order to answer this question, we will need to characterize the economic model cultivated in Georgia.

Based on statistical data about Georgia's economy, we can assume that the consumer economic model has been formed in Georgia. In order to prove this, it would be enough to point out that imports, unfortunately, have been exceeding exports by 3.5 times for a number of years now, while the share of imported goods in the consumer basket, as well as the food basket, consistently reaches about 80 percent. In other words, we consume more than we produce. And if this is so, the natural question is, how do we manage to do that? The answer is definitely not difficult. Specifically, we have two sources of such consumption: remittances from abroad and bank loans.

After the restoration of independence, numerous of our compatriots left Georgia in various periods and for various reasons. Establishing their more-or-less precise number is quite difficult; however, it must be pointed out that for a number of years, Georgia has been consistently receiving about USD 1–1.5 billion annually through various banking channels. The information about this is recorded by the National Bank of Georgia. This is part of the money earned by our compatriots abroad and sent to their relatives for subsistence here in Georgia. As it turns out, our compatriots who left the country work for the economic development of other countries, and through parts of income generated there, they feed their relatives in their homeland. This is an important source where our citizens are facilitating consumption.

As for bank loans, this is a separate phenomenon. Important credit resources for Georgian banks are low-interest loans taken on the European financial market and placed in Georgia with a relatively high interest rate. Back in the period of the governance of the United National Movement, the system of almost coercive distribution of consumer loans was being utilized. Almost all household appliances shops (TV, fridge, mobile phone, etc.) offered loans to all potential customers in order to help them buy their appliances.

Given that household appliances are not being produced in Georgia and are wholly imported, Georgia practically turned into a financial pipeline where credit resources brought from abroad are used by our citizens to consume imported goods. The financial resources attracted from abroad are going to third countries that produce the household appliances. Hence, Georgia intensively consumes things that it does not produce, using money that was not generated in our country. This has been complemented by the debts easily taken by our citizens for various purposes—debts that they have turned out to be unable to pay.

The prime minister of Georgia, Mamuka Bakhtadze, publicly stated that too much indebtedness is suffocating the country, as about 630,000 people (almost 32 percent of the active labor force of our country) are on the so-called blacklist, meaning they have problems with servicing or repaying their loans. It is also worth noting that foreign direct investments entering Georgia are mostly concentrated on the purchases of real estate and are seldom used in the development of the real sector of the economy. All this creates a predicament when the real sector of the Georgian economy, due to underdevelopment, is not the main generator of the population's income. Unfortunately, as pointed out earlier, its function is taken over by remittances from abroad and loans.

In such a situation, the vision of the government for the economic development of the country and the economic policies exercised by the state are of utmost importance. Unfortunately, beginning from the period of the United National Movement, the government was mostly focused on the development of tourism in our country. Equally regrettably, the Georgian Dream government does not seem to have a different vision; it also puts special emphasis on increasing Georgia's fame and attractiveness among tourists.

It is well known that tourism is a driving force of the real sector of the economy. However, this premise needs clarification in the Georgian case, as tourism in Georgia fails to serve as a development force for the country's underdeveloped economy. In reality, tourism in Georgia develops the real sectors of the economies of the countries from where it gets most of its imports. And this is not very surprising if we remember that no more than 20 percent of the consumer basket in Georgia is actually produced in the country; the remaining 80 percent is imported. Tourists visiting Georgia utilize the same consumer basket, of course. Consequently, as more tourists visit Georgia, the country has to import (in absolute dimensions) more.

It would not be correct to give the reader an impression that I am principally opposed to the facilitation of tourism development. In reality, tourism is a very important part of the economies of countries where the fields of the real sector of the economy are well-developed. The best instances of this are Switzerland, France, the UK, and the USA, which are not just touristic countries but also boast various highly developed sectors of the economy.

Pronouncing tourism a main priority for the development of our country creates an illusion that the economy is growing while the economic and social situation of the population does not improve. While growing in this way, the Georgian economy not only cannot develop but is, in some sense, being degraded, as this kind of economy does not need highly qualified, creative people occupied with intellectual work. Such people are forced to seek opportunities for utilizing their talents in other countries. As unfortunate as it is, it is a fact that for a number of years, Georgia finds itself in a tourist trap, with the economy growing but not developing.

In order to free the country from this tourist trap, it is important for the government of Georgia to amend the main priority of our country's economy. Specifically, a knowledge-based economy must be declared a priority. This will only become possible if the government makes the fields of education and science the real priorities of development. It is also compulsory for the government's vision to focus on developing the real sector of the economy through industrialization. For this, it is necessary to renew and enrich the socioeconomic development strategy confirmed by the government of Georgia in 2014, entitled "Georgia 2020."

It is regrettable that the government forgot about this document immediately after confirming it. It has not been implemented, but it has not been abolished either. According to the renewed document, each governmental structure must formulate an annual action plan and implement it to achieve inclusive economic growth, with the ultimate goal of creating a knowledge-based economy.

Depreciation of the Georgian National Currency: Economic, Psychological, Administrative, and Political Factors

September 17, 2018[*]

Not only in Georgia but in general, it has become a tendency of governments and the media to turn to economists only when the country, the region, or the world is facing economic difficulties or, even worse, a crisis. Ostensibly, this might be the only positive outcome during troubling economic times, and only for representatives of the profession at that.

In the last four years, economists in Georgia have only seen the limelight when the national currency—the lari (GEL)

---

[*] V. Papava, "Depreciation of the Georgian National Currency: Economic, Psychological, Administrative, and Political Factors," *Rondeli Blog*, September 17, 2018, https://www.gfsis.org/blog/view/864.

—is struggling. Although research (Anguridze, Charaia and Doghonadze 2015) was conducted as early as 2015 with regard to the lari's devaluation, and relevant recommendations were issued, no substantial steps have been taken in this regard. The problem remains acute.

Against the background of a fluctuating national currency exchange rate, the balance of payments—a comprising component of which is the current account, including the balance of trade of goods and services—is very important for the stability of the GEL. For the stability of a national currency, especially for a developing country, the ratio between the country's export and import is critical. The former brings foreign currency into the country, and the latter requires the currency to leave the country. The balance between the two creates the economic basis for the stability of the national currency.

According to 2017 data, import was 3.8 times greater than export (excluding re-export) in Georgia. This, in turn, is the number-one reason why the GEL does not have a strong economic basis for stability.

It is true that the number of tourists arriving in Georgia and the foreign currency they spend here is growing; however, we should not forget that on average, 80 percent of this currency flows out of the country due to the undeveloped real sector of the national economy, where the ratio between imported and domestic products for both consumer as well as the food basket is 4:1. In other words, an average of 80 percent of the amount spent by each tourist flows out of the country to import the products required by this tourist for consumption (Papava 2018). Admittedly, due to the large amounts of money spent by tourists during the tourist season, the absolute value of the 20 percent they leave in the country is growing. But as soon as the season ends, the funds substantially decrease as well.

Besides this, the stability of the GEL is heavily influenced by the stability (or instability) of the respective national currencies of Georgia's main trading partner nations. Georgia's main trading partners are Turkey, Russia, Azerbaijan, and Ukraine. Specifically, combined imports from these countries amounted to 37.3 percent of total imports in 2017. Unfortunately, in recent years, these countries have been characterized by a devaluation of their respective national currencies. In turn, and in line with the basic principles of economics, this promotes the growth of exports, as exporters want to acquire as much foreign currency as they can and as quickly as possible due to the devaluation of their own national currency.

Georgia's two primary trading partners account for more than a quarter of total imports. The national currencies of these two countries—the Turkish lira (TRY) and the Russian ruble (RUB)—are and have been experiencing virtually irreversible devaluation in recent years. The reasons for this include the strengthening of authoritarian tendencies in the governing systems of the countries as well as their confrontations with the United States.

It should be noted that Georgia has had a free trade agreement (FTA) with its main trading partner, Turkey, since 2008. However, this FTA is unambiguously unfair. There are

Becoming European

far fewer barriers imposed on goods imported from Turkey to Georgia than there are on goods exported from Georgia to Turkey (EI-LAT 2011). In this context, the devaluation of the TRY stimulates the growth of Turkish product imports in Georgia; however, in reality, the depreciation rate of the GEL is much quicker and greater than the actual growth of the aforementioned imports due to this devaluation. The reasons for this are no longer economics. This is brought on by psychological and administrative factors.

In the last few years, businesses and, frankly, the entire population of Georgia have been characterized by a tendency to expect an inevitable depreciation of the GEL as soon as information spreads about the depreciation of the TRY or the RUB. This expectation increases the demand for US dollars (USD), which accelerates the depreciation of the GEL even further, despite the fact that due to the depreciation of the TRY or the RUB, imports from these countries grow.

Taking advantage of these psychological factors is nothing short of the modus operandi of commercial banks. Keeping in mind that two large banks hold the dominant position in the Georgian banking system, their behavior requires special attention. In particular, it has been substantiated on numerous occasions that precisely these banks have been the initiators of a spasmodic increase in the demand for the USD or GEL on the currency market, especially and specifically when information is spread about the depreciation of the TRY or RUB. The chiefs of these banks understand well that the depreciation of the GEL will be "blamed" not on them but on the depreciation of these foreign currencies. As a result, large-scale banks receive additional profits from these speculative operations. And here we have come to the administrative factor.

Supervision of the banking sector is bestowed upon the National Bank of Georgia (NBG); however, it has never had a conflict or been at odds with these large banks. Furthermore, suspicion has taken root in Georgian society (not without reason) that it is not the NBG that carries out supervision of these two large banks but, rather, it is these banks that dictate actions to the management of the NBG.

Unfortunately, even when currency fluctuations are clearly noticeable and when the GEL is experiencing leaping devaluations, the NBG often chooses to remain silent, as if the fate of the GEL is of no concern to it, instead of trying to calm the currency market with public announcements. With such actions (or more accurately, a lack thereof), it unfortunately promotes elements of panic in the market.

The NBG has numerous tools and instruments at its disposal to curtail the drastic depreciation of the GEL, but the bank uses them far too late in the best-case scenario and, in the worst-case, not at all. Currency reserves, for example, are intended to alleviate just such a crisis. When the GEL is depreciating, using these reserves in small doses is necessary not to maintain the exchange rate at what it is (that would be a mistake!) but to avoid leaps and bounds in the depreciation. This could and should be a useful tool for the prevention of possible panic on the currency market.

The inflation targeting—which the NBG implements obediently according to recommendations of the International Monetary Fund (IMF)—represents a separate problem. At this time, no one can argue with Nobel laureate in economics Joseph E. Stiglitz in his claim that in countries where import significantly exceeds export, an inflation targeting is not viable, and the corresponding monetary policy is a failure (Stiglitz 2008). Sadly, the IMF's bureaucracy is blind to this argument, nor does the leadership of the NBG adhere to the argumentation of Joseph Stiglitz and other renowned economists (Weber 2015). This is especially noteworthy considering Georgia's imports are 3.8 times its exports.

Lastly, it is necessary to say at least a few words on the political component of the problem. It is unfortunate but nevertheless true that the depreciation of the GEL is beneficial to the political opposition, especially when this depreciation is turbulent in character and leads to substantial discontent among businesses and the general population. This is not surprising, as the devaluation of the GEL allows for criticism of the ruling political party and the government's economic policies.

Regrettably, the political opposition does not consider the role of the NBG at all, since this does not meet its political interests. If we consider that the parent of the GEL is the NBG, then first and foremost, the NBG should be held accountable for the stability of the GEL and only afterward the government. Lamentably, the government administration plays into the hands of these opposition games when its finance and economic ministers and their deputies make comments on the devaluation of the currency while NBG officials fail to utter a word.

What is happening around the GEL is due to many objective and subjective factors. All require a deliberate and consistent solution.

References

Anguridze, O., V. Charaia, and I. Doghonadze. 2015. *Security Problems & Modern Challenges of the Georgian National Currency*. Tbilisi: Tbilisi University Press.

EI-LAT. 2011. *Georgian-Turkish Free Trade Agreement 2008: Implications Two Years After*. Tbilisi: The European Initiative Liberal Academy Tbilisi.

Papava, V. 2018. "Georgia's Economy in a "Tourist Trap"." *Rondeli Blog*, July 25, https://www.gfsis.org/blog/view/854 (last accessed September 10, 2018).

Stiglitz, J. E. 2008. "The Failure of Inflation Targeting." *Project Syndicate*, May 17, https://www.project-syndicate.org/commentary/the-failure-of-inflation-targeting?barrier=accesspaylog (last accessed September 10, 2018).

Weber, A. 2015. "Rethinking Inflation Targeting." *Project Syndicate*, June 8, https://www.project-syndicate.org/commentary/rethinking-inflation-targeting-price-stability-by-axel-weber-1-2015-06?barrier=accesspaylog (last accessed September 10, 2018).

Why Georgia Needs Economists
October 12, 2018[*]

In 2018, Georgia is celebrating the hundredth anniversary of the Democratic Republic, as well as one hundred years of the establishment of the first university in the Caucasus, Tbilisi State University. It was also one hundred years ago, on September 13, 1918, that the first Georgian periodical, a scientific journal entitled *Georgia's Economist,* was published, marking a particularly important event for Georgian economists. In fact, the systematic scientific-research activities of economists in Georgia begins with the publishing of this journal. Today, multiple scientific journals dedicated to the field of economics are being published in the country, including some that are incorporated into international scientific databases.

---

[*] V. Papava, "Why Georgia Needs Economists." *Rondeli Blog*, October 12, 2018, https://www.gfsis.org/blog/view/864.

Given this background, the reader might find the title of this post somewhat peculiar. However, we believe that the actual situation in Georgia requires just this sort of analysis. For the past ten to fifteen years, Georgia has been dominated by the view that governing the country requires not economists but managers.

In January 2013, during his meeting with experts, the prime minister of Georgia categorically stated that he is not interested in listening to economists, he does not require relations with them, and that for him, it is much more interesting to listen to a political scientist talking about economic issues. His attitude was reflected by the government's economic team and that of the parliament, where professional economists are rarely appointed to positions. In today's Georgia, this problem has become even more severe. There are no places for economists within leading cabinet (governmental) positions.

The management attitude in governing the country is not at all new in Georgia. It has its origins in the late period of Eduard Shevardnadze's presidency when the then minister of finance, who was a physicist by training (and who managed to retain this position in Mikheil Saakashvili's government as well and later even became prime minister), boasted that he was serving as a "good manager" in the cabinet.

In all fairness, it must be pointed out that during his presidency, especially at the beginning, Eduard Shevardnadze used to invite professional economists to high political offices in his government's economic team. Most of them were from the halls of academia. For Mikheil Saakashvili, meanwhile,

Becoming European

academia was unacceptable almost on principle. He even purposefully tried to destroy this field. He constructed a cabinet mostly of people who were loyal to him and who, in most cases, were nonprofessionals.

The elevation of libertarian ideas to the status of government policy in Georgia during Mikheil Saakashvili's presidency is connected to the appointment of a businessman from Moscow, Kakha Bendukidze (a biologist by training), to the position of the minister of the economy. In reality, the policies implemented in Georgia at that time can be described as pseudo-libertarianism. The ideology of libertarianism was selected only because there were no professional economists in the government. They did not know what the real problems in the economy were. In order to hide one's lack of knowledge of economics, the easiest path is to admit that the government must not intervene in the economy. In addition, the so-called Georgian Libertarians were ignoring the systemic violation of property rights in the country, which is why libertarianism became a dominant ideology in Georgia although in practice, pseudo-libertarianism (Papava 2014) was established.

During Bidzina Ivanishvili's premiership, professional economists from academia once again appeared in the government of Georgia, but unfortunately, they remain as the "last of the Mohicans" in the team. As an achievement of this period we can consider the creation of a social-economic strategic document, entitled "Georgia 2020." In fact, the measures put forward by this document were disregarded very quickly when the minister of economy, possessing the diplomas of a physician and a manager, was appointed to the position of prime minister and quickly replaced the aforementioned professionally sound document with a primitive four-point plan (Papava 2017).

Back in 1996, a Nobel Prize winner in economics, Paul Krugman, published a noteworthy article entitled *A Country Is Not a Company*. Unfortunately, the arguments about why a country is not a company still elude the political leadership of Georgia, who continue the hiring practices of the Saakashvili period and appoint managers and not economists (including, once again, a physician) to high-level positions in the government.

The very basis of any country's development is improving the quality of the life of its population and achieving stable economic development and inclusive economic growth. As for a company, its vital driver is increasing its profit and/or value. This is the main difference between the criteria for assessing the goals and success of a country and a company.

This is where the difference between *public administration* and *business administration* stems. It is noteworthy that in accordance with the established practices in almost all leading universities in the world, Georgian universities also train students in these two directions. The government needs leaders who are professional governors in their respective fields. The place for managers is in businesses, and they should not have anything to do with the government.

One of the products of the government's managerial vision is the prioritizing of tourism (Papava 2018) as a main sector of the country's economic development and the production of marijuana as a raw material for export (CG 2018). In reality, the country requires the creation and development of a knowledge-based economy (EPID 2015) as well industrialization of the economy (Ross 2018).

Even if the government's economic team consisted of professional economists, it would still be important for the leader of the country to have a council of economic experts as an advisory body. Given the fact that there are no professional economists within the government's economic team, the existence of such a council becomes even more important for formulating correct economic policies. It is a well-known fact that US President Harry Truman created the Council of Economic Advisors (CEA 2018) back in 1946. This council consisted and still consists of famous economists from the halls of academia and continues to deliver professional advice to the president on issues pertaining to the country's economy.

Many might not know that on a distant autumn in 1920, the government of the Democratic Republic of Georgia prepared a unique document entitled "Statute of the Republic's High Economic Council." Unfortunately, Georgia's government was unable to implement this document due to the Russian occupation of February 23, 1921. Head of the Georgian State Eduard Shevardnadze created an economic council in 1993; however, the Georgian model was far from perfect, as apart from professional economists, it also included the ministers of the government's economic team. Hence, the council had more of a political character than a professional one.

In 2005, President Mikheil Saakashvili also created this type of council, which consisted solely of professional economists. Unfortunately, the council held only one session, in March 2005. For the rest of his presidential term, Saakashvili, who was chairman of the council, never convened it or tasked it with anything again, although he did not abolish it either.

The Georgian Dream came to power after the 2012 parliamentary elections. At the end of 2013, they created an economic council as an advisory body to the prime minister. It is noteworthy that the council consisted solely of leading officials from the government. Not even a single place was allocated for economists from academia. On the anniversary of the creation of the council, its statute was updated, but it still does not include any economists from academia.

The function of this type of council is unjustified due to its members, who, as government officials, are already at the disposal of the prime minister. This affords him no opportunity for learning about differing opinions, let alone alternative options.

In order for the country's economic policy to be successful, it needs to be formulated by a team of professional economists (not managers) employed by the government and the prime minister, who has extensive powers in Georgia, as the country is a parliamentary republic. The prime minister must be given the opportunity to get independent counsel from professional economists from academia. In order to do this, it would be advisable to consider the US experience and create a council of economic advisors consisting of professional economists.

References

CEA. 2018. *Council of Economic Advisors*, https://www.whitehouse.gov/cea/ (last accessed October 7, 2018).

CG. 2018. "Govt Mulls Medical Cannabis Cultivation for Export." *Civil Georgia*, September 11, https://civil.ge/archives/253652 (last accessed October 7, 2018).

EPID. 2015. "Knowledge-Based Economy." *European Portal of Integration and Development*, http://europejskiportal.eu/knowledge-based-economy/ (last accessed October 7, 2018).

Krugman, P. 1996. "A Country is Not a Company." *Harvard Business Review*, January–February, https://hbr.org/1996/01/a-country-is-not-a-company (last accessed October 7, 2018).

Papava, V. 2014. "The Georgian Model of Libertarianism and Its Applicability to Ukraine." *Democracy & Freedom Watch*, September 29, https://dfwatch.net/the-georgian-model-of-libertarianism-and-its-applicability-to-ukraine-53714-31393 (last accessed October 7, 2018).

Papava, V., 2017. *Georgia's Economy: From Optimism to Primitivism*. GFSIS Expert Opinion, 75. Tilisi: Georgian Foundation for Strategic and International Studies, https://www.gfsis.org/files/library/opinion-papers/75-expert-opinion-eng.pdf (last accessed October 7, 2018).

Papava, V. 2018. "Georgia's Economy in a "Tourist Trap"." *Rondeli Blog*, July 25, https://www.gfsis.org/blog/view/854 (last accessed September 10, 2018).

Ross, S. 2018. "How Can Industrialization Affect National Economies of LDCs?" *Investopedia*, June 5, https://www.investopedia.com/ask/answers/042015/how-can-industrialization-affect-national-economy-less-developed-countries-ldcs.asp (last accessed September 10, 2018).

30

Why the Population of Georgia Does Not Perceive Economic Growth Positively

November 30, 2018[*]

For the past two years, the Georgian economy has been experiencing moderate economic growth. While GDP growth amounted to 2.8 percent in 2016, it had already increased to 4.9 percent in 2017. The growth of GDP in the first half of 2018 is already 5.4 percent. Despite this, polling (CRRC Georgia 2018) suggests that public attitude toward the government's economic policies remains negative. We often hear that economic growth is not being reflected in the welfare of citizens or that the country is developing in a wrong direction. In order to examine this issue, we must separate the

---

[*] V. Papava, "Why the Population of Georgia does not Perceive Economic Growth Positively," *Rondeli Blog*, November 30, 2018, https://www.gfsis.org/blog/view/888.

problems that generally characterize GDP indicators from the problems of incorrect economic policy in Georgia.

It should be stated from the outset that most economists today agree that GDP provides a very rough image of the economic situation and is not much use for assessing the welfare of individuals. This is illustrated by a report initiated by the president of France, Nicholas Sarkozy, and produced by an authoritative commission of economists parallel to the global financial and economic crisis. The commission was led by two Nobel Prize winners in economics, Joseph E. Stiglitz and Amartya Sen, and the famous French economist Jean-Paul Fitoussi. The unique report (Stiglitz, Sen and Fitoussi 2009) they prepared explains why the GDP indicator does not provide enough information to make correct decisions.

The report of the aforementioned commission presents numerous clear examples of times when GDP not only does not reflect the increase in human welfare but rather GDP growth is sometimes actually caused by the reduction of human welfare. For instance, the higher the number of road accidents, the higher the GDP. More specifically, if road infrastructure is damaged, the cost of repairs as well as the cost of repairing damaged vehicles, the expenditure necessary for treatment of persons involved in the accident, and, in the case of death, the cost of funerals, are added to the GDP.

The fact that the GDP indicator cannot describe human welfare is no longer debated among economists, and there have been multiple attempts to create alternative indicators reflecting different aspects of human well-being. One such indicator is the Human Development Index (UNDP 2018). The Happiness Index (Helliwell, Layard, and Sachs 2018), which is becoming more popular each year, should also be mentioned. Despite the diversity of such indicators, economists still believe that refusing to use GDP at all would be a mistake. Despite its many flaws, GDP still manages to assess economic growth on a certain level. At the same time, we must always remember that this growth does not necessarily equal a growth in human well-being.

As already stated, what fuels economic growth in Georgia is a whole separate issue. Delving into this will enable us to explain why the population does not perceive economic growth positively. With economic growth in the first quarter of 2018 at 5.3 percent as compared to the same period of the previous year, especially high growth was recorded in economic activities such as mining and quarrying, 11.4 percent; electricity, gas, and water supply, 10 percent; hotels and restaurants, 10.9. percent; financial intermediation, 9.1 percent; real estate, renting, and business activities, 13.4 percent; other community, social, and personal service activities, 13.4 percent; and financial intermediation services indirectly measured, 13.6 percent.

As you can see, the areas of high growth tend to be economic activities that do not have an impact on the well-being of citizens. Specifically, this includes financial intermediation, real estate operations, renting, and consumer service and financial intermediation services, indirectly measured. As for economic growth in the field of hospitality (hotels and restaurants), this is mainly caused by the development of tourism. Given Georgia's negative trade balance and the quadruple amount of imported goods as compared to locally produced ones in consumer and food baskets, this is pulling the country toward a tourist trap (Papava 2018a).

This ugly situation, characteristic of the current stage of Georgia's economic development, escalated in the second quarter of 2018. More specifically, the growth of GDP in this period was 5.5 percent as compared to the same period of 2017, while financial intermediation, for example, increased by 22 percent and financial intermediation services indirectly measured increased by 19.9 percent. Thus the negative trends characteristic to the first quarter of 2018 have become even more pronounced in the second quarter.

When an economic activity, such as financial intermediation, grows at such an excessive rate, it must not be surprising to us that the main problem facing about 630,000 Georgian citizens is overindebtedness. According to the statement by Prime Minister Mamuka Bakhtadze, a large part of the population spends 25 to 30 percent, or even as much as 40 percent, of their income on servicing loans. Naturally, given such conditions, the pronounced growth of a factor of GDP such as financial intermediation does in no way improve the welfare of citizens.

In order for economic growth to be more or less positively reflected on human welfare, it is necessary for the economy of the country to move to an inclusive growth (Arevadze 2015) model that requires more citizen involvement in production and which was correctly underlined in the document of the strategy of Georgia's social-economic development: "Georgia 2020." Unfortunately, this document, confirmed by the government of Georgia in 2014, was soon forgotten and was never implemented (Papava 2018b).

The initiative of the government of Georgia to build an electric-car factory should be seen as heartening. It is exactly these kinds of projects that will facilitate not only inclusive economic growth but also the industrialization of our country by creating and developing a knowledge-based economy. For the latter, it will be vitally important to implement many such projects and to prioritize the funding of science and university education at a government policy level.

References

Arevadze, L. 2015. "What is Inclusive Growth?" *Institute for Development of Freedom of Information (IDFI)*, December 15, https://idfi.ge/en/what-is-inclusive-growth (last accessed November 27, 2018).

CRRC Georgia. 2018. "Public Attitudes in Georgia Results of March 2018 Survey Carried Out for NDI by CRRC Georgia." *NDI*, https://www.ndi.org/sites/default/files/NDI_March_2018_Public%20Presentation_English_final.pdf (last accessed November 27, 2018).

Helliwell, J., R. Layard, and J. Sachs. 2018. *World Happiness Report 2018*. New York: Sustainable Development Solutions Network https://worldhappiness.report/ed/2018/ (last accessed November 27, 2018).

Papava, V. 2018a. "Georgia's Economy in a "Tourist Trap"." *Rondeli Blog*, July 25, https://www.gfsis.org/blog/view/854 (last accessed November 27, 2018).

Papava, V. 2018b. "Why Georgia Needs Economists." *Rondeli Blog*, October 12, https://www.gfsis.org/blog/view/864.

Stiglitz, J. E., A. Sen, and J.-P. Fitoussi. 2009. *Report by the Commission on the Measurement of Economic Performance and Social Progress*. September 16, https://web.archive.org/web/20150721025729/http://www.stiglitz-sen-fitoussi.fr/documents/rapport_anglais.pdf (last accessed November 27, 2018).

UNDP. 2018. "Human Development Index (HDI)." *United Nations Development Programme*, http://hdr.undp.org/en/content/human-development-index-hdi (last accessed November 27, 2018).

31

Whither Economic Policy?

November 25, 2019[*]

In the contemporary world, it is impossible to find a country that does not have a more or less severe confrontation between economic policymakers and academic economists. Post-Communist Georgia is no exception to this. In such a situation, the question of why this conflict has arisen in the first place must be answered.

The essence of the problem is that quite often, economic policy is not simply distanced from economics but, in certain cases, even in conflict with its basic tenets. Such an economic policy that is not in convergence with economics we would call a *noneconomic economic policy* or, to make it even shorter, *noneconomic policy*.

---

[*] V. Papava, "Whither Economic Policy?" *Rondeli Blog*, November 25, 2019. https://www.gfsis.org/blog/view/1000.

In order to determine the main source of the primacy of noneconomic policy, it is necessary to consider three types:

1. Those who determine economic policies do not take the knowledge created by economic science into account.
2. Economic policymakers do heed the knowledge created by economic science, yet the knowledge itself is false.
3. Economic science has not yet studied certain important economic phenomena, hence economic policymakers would be unable to utilize the hitherto nonexistent knowledge, even if they were highly motivated to do so.

The first type of noneconomic policy could arise because the economic policymakers are not professional economists or are economists of extremely low qualification and, therefore, are not sufficiently familiar with the achievements of economic science but sometimes also even with the basics of economics. It could also occur because the economic policymakers may be sufficiently qualified economists but do not find it beneficial to reflect on the achievements of economics in economic policy.

It is noteworthy that politicians very often look at their country as though it were a company, which is why it is considered that the key positions determining economic policy must be filled with managers rather than professional economists (Papava 2018b). A famous article by a Nobel Prize-winning economist, Paul Krugman, entitled "A Country Is

Not a Company" (Krugman 1996), clearly shows that there are principled differences between a country and a company. Regrettably, a large number of politicians do not realize this. In reality, the place for managers (not to mention businessmen themselves) is in business, not politics.

When the governing persons authorized to make political decisions in the field of economics do not possess a specified economics education, their lack of knowledge is usually compensated by the professionalism of the individuals who prepare draft decisions for the governors. However, even in this case, it is entirely possible to get a situation where the governors of economic policy, despite the abovementioned drafts, will only consider political viability when making decisions.

Even when the governing persons authorized to make decisions regarding economic policy do in fact have an economics education, it is still oftentimes the case that they do not use the knowledge accumulated by economics when making decisions but rather base them entirely on the considerations of political advisability. This phenomenon of political viability being prioritized over economic science during the formulation of economic policy is explained by the world-renowned Public Choice theory (Buchanan and Tullock 1998).

The cause of the second type of noneconomic policy is the mistakes made by economic science itself. According to the Nobel Prize-winning economist Joseph Stiglitz, the 2007–2009 global financial and economic crisis is a clear example of this (Stiglitz 2010). More specifically, the approaches of economic science toward economic regulations turned out to be incorrect (Cliffe 2019). The connections between economic science and economic policy (or, more precisely, public policy) can be compared to the links between biology and medicine or physics and engineering on the basis of which a conclusion is reached. If a mistake is made in medicine, this is not the fault of biology, just as it would be unjustified to blame physics for the mistakes made in engineering (Hausmann 2019). I believe that such an interpretation is not fully correct, since if the root of the mistake turned out to be within biology, it would consequently show up in medicine as well.

A clear example of the third type of noneconomic policy is the transition from a command economy to a market economy in the absence of an appropriate economic theory. The phenomenon of the dissemination of cryptocurrencies around the world when economic science has yet to create a more-or-less grounded theory about them is no less noteworthy. According to the Nobel Prize–winning economist Robert Shiller, the economic mechanism for the emission of cryptocurrencies remains unclear to this day (Shiller 2018). Despite this, the former managing director of the International Monetary Fund and the current president of the European Central Bank, Christine Lagarde, is optimistic about the future of cryptocurrencies (Lagarde 2017). This creates a danger that the third type of noneconomic policy will be formed with regard to cryptocurrencies.

It is notable that at the beginning of the post-Communist transformation of economies, the third type of noneconomic policy was taking place before the period of transition to a market economy was concluded. Thereafter, the first type of noneconomic policy has been brought to the forefront. This is confirmed by the experiences of post-Communist Georgia too.

At the beginning of 1992, radical economic reforms started to be undertaken using the Polish version of the well-known shock therapy. More specifically, the so-called Balcerowicz Plan (EB 2019) was used, which owes its name to its author, Leszek Balcerowicz, the vice prime minister and minister of finance of Poland at the end of the 1980s and the beginning of the 1990s. For Georgia, however, the Balcerowicz Plan was destined to fail from the outset, since at that time, unlike Russia and Poland, Georgia did not have one of the main instruments of shock therapy: its own currency.

After the so-called Rose Revolution of 2003, the supremacy of libertarian views (ESI 2010) in the economic policy of the government of Georgia is connected to the name of Kakha Bendukidze, who arrived in Georgia from Moscow at the invitation of the government. The economic policy of Georgian Libertarianism (Papava 2014) was based on the abolition of a large number of licenses and permits necessary for starting a business, the reduction of the tax burden, and so on.

Parallel to the supposedly libertarian reforms, the United National Movement government violated human rights (HRIDC 2004), limited the independence of media (HRIDC 2008a), and systematically violated property rights (HRIDC 2008b), by which it managed to perform a forced redistribution of property (Rimple 2012). Taking these factors into account, unfortunately, the reforms undertaken by the then government of Georgia carried the façade of a libertarian nature, yet according to my position as well as that of other researchers, it was neo-Bolshevik (de Waal 2011) in its content. It is clear that Georgian Libertarianism, in essence, is a type-one noneconomic policy.

From 2016, the economic policy of the government of Georgia was based on the four-point plan of the government, which was a clear example of economic primitivism (Papava 2017b), as it did not at all envisage the development of the real sector of the economy and was mainly oriented on developing tourism (Papava 2018a) in Georgia.

An even clearer example of economic primitivism is the privatization of the building of the Ministry of Economy and Sustainable Development of Georgia, which took place in 2015. As a result, to this day, the ministry is forced to rent a building (Papava 2017a).

On the contemporary stage of economic development, it is especially important for Georgia to formulate and implement an economic policy that will be based on the achievements of economic science, for which it is necessary for the government to intensively cooperate with economists (Papava 2018b).

References

Buchanan, J. M. and G. Tullock. 1998. *The Calculus of Consent: Logical Foundations of Constitutional Democracy*, https://www.

econlib.org/library/Buchanan/buchCv3.html (last accessed November 21, 2019).

Cliffe, M. 2019. "What Economists Still Need to Learn." *Project Syndicate*, September 9, https://www.project-syndicate.org/commentary/macroeconomic-models-three-lessons-2008-crisis-by-mark-cliffe-2019-09?utm_source=Project%20Syndicate%20Newsletter&utm_campaign=aabf9c90ac-sunday_newsletter_15_9_2019&utm_medium=email&utm_term=0_73bad5b7d8-aabf9c90ac-93567601&mc_cid=aabf9c90ac&mc_eid=e9fb6cbcc0&barrier=accesspaylog (last accessed November 21, 2019).

de Waal, T. 2011. *Georgia's Choices: Charting a Future in Uncertain Times*. Washington, D.C.: Carnegie Endowment, https://carnegieendowment.org/files/georgias_choices.pdf (last accessed November 21, 2019).

EB. 2019. "Balcerowicz Plan." *Encyclopædia Britannica*, https://www.britannica.com/topic/Balcerowicz-Plan (last accessed November 21, 2019).

ESI. 2010. *Reinventing Georgia: The Story of a Libertarian Revolution*. Berlin–Brussels–Istanbul: European Stability Initiative, https://www.esiweb.org/index.php?lang=en&id=322&debate_ID=3 (last accessed November 21, 2019).

Hausmann, R. 2019. "Don't Blame Economics, Blame Public Policy." *Project Syndicate*, September 1, https://www.project-syndicate.org/commentary/blame-public-policy-not-economics-by-ricardo-hausmann-2019-08?utm_source=Project%20Syndicate%20Newsletter&utm_campaign=d58b1700af-sunday_newsletter_8_9_2019&utm_medium=email&utm_term=0_73bad5b7d8-d58b1700af-93567601&mc_cid=d58b1700af&mc_eid=e9fb6cbcc0&barrier=accesspaylog (last accessed November 21, 2019).

HRIDC. 2004. *One Step Forward, Two Steps Back: Human Rights in Georgia after the "Rose Revolution."* Tbilisi: Human Rights Information and Documentation Center, http://www.humanrights.ge/files/REPORT.pdf (last accessed November 21, 2019).

HRIDC. 2008a. *Putinization of Georgia: Georgian Media after the Rose Revolution Media in Georgia 2003-2007.* Tbilisi: Human Rights Information and Documentation Center, http://www.humanrights.ge/admin/editor/uploads/files/Georgian%20Media%20after%20the%20Rose%20revolution.pdf (last accessed November 21, 2019).

HRIDC. 2008b. *The Big Eviction. Violations of Property Rights in Georgia.* Tbilisi: Human Rights Information and Documentation Center, http://www.humanrights.ge/admin/editor/uploads/files/Big%20Eviction.pdf (last accessed November 21, 2019).

Krugman, P. 1996. "A Country is Not a Company." *Harvard Business Review*, January–February, https://hbr.org/1996/01/a-country-is-not-a-company (last accessed November 21, 2019).

Lagarde, C. 2017. "Central Banking and Fintech—A Brave New World?" *International Monetary Fund*, September 29, https://www.imf.org/en/News/Articles/2017/09/28/sp092917-central-banking-and-fintech-a-brave-new-world?cid=em-COM-123-35955 (last accessed November 21, 2019).

Papava, V. 2014. "The Georgian Model of Libertarianism and Its Applicability to Ukraine." *Democracy & Freedom Watch*, September 29, https://dfwatch.net/the-georgian-model-of-libertarianism-and-its-applicability-to-ukraine-53714-31393 (last accessed November 21, 2019).

Papava, V. 2017a. "Features of Governmental 'Business' in Post-Soviet Georgia." *Eurasia Review*, June 27, https://www.eurasiareview.

com/27062017-features-of-governmental-business-in-post-soviet-georgia-oped/.

Papava, V. 2017b. "Primitivism as a Trait of Georgia's Modern Economic Policy." *Central Asia-Caucasus Analyst*, May 4, http://cacianalyst.org/publications/analytical-articles/item/13444-primitivism-as-a-trait-of-georgia%E2%80%99s-modern-economic-policy.html.

Papava, V. 2018a. "Georgia's Economy in a "Tourist Trap"." *Rondeli Blog*, July 25, https://www.gfsis.org/blog/view/854 (last accessed November 21, 2019).

Papava, V. 2018b. "Why Georgia Needs Economists." *Rondeli Blog*, October 12, https://www.gfsis.org/blog/view/864 (last accessed November 21, 2019).

Rimple, P. 2012. *Who Owned Georgia 2003-2012*. Tbilisi: Transparency International Georgia, https://www.transparency.ge/sites/default/files/post_attachments/Who%20Owned%20Georgia%20English.pdf (last accessed November 21, 2019).

Shiller, R. J. 2018. "The Old Allure of New Money." *Project Syndicate*, May 21, https://www.project-syndicate.org/commentary/cryptocurrencies-scientific-narrative-by-robert-j--shiller-2018-05?utm_source=Project%20Syndicate%20Newsletter&utm_campaign=c4c50cbed2-sunday_newsletter_27_5_2018&utm_medium=email&utm_term=0_73bad5b7d8-c4c50cbed2-93567601&barrier=accesspaylog (last accessed November 21, 2019).

Stiglitz, J. E. 2010. "Joseph Stiglitz in the Financial Times on the Need for a New Economic Paradigm." *Institute for New Economic Thinking*, August 18, https://www.ineteconomics.org/about/news/2010/joseph-stiglitz-in-the-financial-times-on-the-need-for-a-new-economic-paradigm (last accessed November 21, 2019).

32

Moscow's Political Trap for Georgia: Stable Instability

March 10, 2020[*]

It is commonly believed that Moscow is interested in seeing openly pro-Russian political parties come to power in former Soviet countries. Armenia, Belarus, Kazakhstan, and Kyrgyzstan are the best examples of this trend in the post-Soviet space. Russia united these countries in the Eurasian Economic Union, which has no economic prospects but instead is driven by political goals (Papava 2015).

In my opinion, it oversimplifies the actual situation to think that the only goal of Moscow is to have political parties with openly pro-Russian orientation govern post-Soviet

---

[*] V. Papava, "Moscow's 'Political Trap' for Georgia: 'Stable Instability,'" *Eurasia Review*, March 10, 2020, https://www.eurasiareview.com/10032020-moscows-political-trap-for-georgia-stable-instability-oped/.

countries. In reality, the situations that have developed in various post-Soviet countries are not homogenous. Therefore, it is necessary that the situations in each post-Soviet country be examined individually.

In this regard, the situation in Georgia is of particular interest. Despite its clearly Euro-Atlantic orientation (Kakachia 2013), Georgia is not free of the so-called pro-Russian phenomenon. As a result, not only do the main opposition parties—United National Movement (UNM) and the European Georgia Movement for Liberty (EGML), which were separated from the UNM—accuse the ruling Georgian Dream (GD) party of being pro-Russian, but the ruling party thinks that the key opposition parties play into the hands of Russia and thus are of pro-Russian orientation as well (Berekashvili 2019).

Notwithstanding the political divorce, the UNM and its splinter party, EGML, easily find a common language, especially in order to oppose the GD. For instance, the UNM and EGML, along with other smaller political parties, supported Grigol Vashadze as a joint candidate in the second round of the 2018 presidential elections (Shlamov 2018). It is not impossible that in the future, the UNM and EGML will be united again, either in an electoral bloc or a parliamentary coalition.

A key argument brought up by the opposition parties to prove that the GD is pro-Russian is that its founder and chairman, Bidzina Ivanishvili, became a billionaire in Russia (Tabula 2012) and that he is still managed by Russian President

Vladimir Putin. The opposition was effective in its criticism of the mistakes the GD made in reforming the judicial and electoral systems. The opposition has been quite successful in persuading even American politicians and friends of Georgia as to the pro-Russian orientation of the GD's party leader (GJ 2020).

The GD's accusation of the UNM and its splinter parties being pro-Russian is based on the support Vladimir Putin provided to Saakashvili in carrying out the Rose Revolution in 2003 (Sindelar 2008); solving the problem in Ajara in 2004 (GMT 2004); and transferring Georgia's strategic facilities to Russia (Papava and Starr 2006)—as well the GD party's references to the mistakes made during the Russia-Georgia war in 2008 (Traynor 2009).

Taking into account that Georgia, which adopted a parliamentary republic model by its constitution, is to hold parliamentary elections in the fall of 2020, it is very important to find out what the expectations of Moscow are vis-à-vis these upcoming elections and what kind of political forces it wants to come to power in Georgia. Moscow's political menu of opposition parties in Georgia is diverse: there is an openly pro-Russian party, the United Georgia Democratic Movement (UGDM), and the Alliance of Patriots of Georgia (APG), which was founded as a patriotic party and at the same time is in favor of active cooperation with Russia. On the other hand, there are publicly pro-Western parties that have a relatively large number of voters: the UNM and the EGML. It is noteworthy that the ruling GD party is also publicly pro-Western.

It is to be underlined that a newly established political party, Lelo, stands out from this political landscape. Its public statements are pro-Western, and the party is not burdened by prior political experience. However, its founders are leaders of one of the largest banks in Georgia (JAMnews 2019), which is perceived in the country to be the main culprit in bankrupting many citizens. Therefore, Lelo probably will find it difficult to achieve significant success in the approaching parliamentary elections.

Given the widespread opinion that Moscow favors an openly pro-Russian party coming to power in Georgia, it can be inferred that the Kremlin made a serious mistake by failing to promote the UGDM at the end of 2019. The chairwoman of this party, Nino Burjanadze, visited Moscow in December in regard to setting free Vazha Gaprindashvili, a Georgian medical doctor who was illegally detained for crossing the Russian occupation line in South Ossetia in November 2019 (CG 2019). Upon returning to Georgia, she announced with great confidence that Russia would release the doctor from illegal detention no later than December 13, 2019 (IPN 2019). If he had been released, Nino Burjanadze's image and popularity would certainly have significantly increased among voters.

In fact, this was not the case. The doctor who was detained by the occupation regime was set free only on December 28, 2019 (RFE/RL's Georgian Service 2019). So the release of Vazha Gaprindashvili from illegal detention cannot be credited to Nino Burjanadze's effort. What, then, does this interesting case, so full of drama, indicate? If it was in Moscow's interest to support an openly pro-Russian political party, Nino Burjanadze would not have been lied to, and as she was promised, Vazha Gaprindashvili would have been released no later than December 13, 2019.

This development should not come as a surprise if we take into consideration the following circumstance. If an openly pro-Russian political party comes to power in Georgia, Moscow will have to make some compromises with Tbilisi. First of all, this would involve restoring the territorial integrity of Georgia, which is definitely not in the interest of Moscow. Russia occupies 20 percent of Georgia's territory (Ellyatt 2019), and that is quite sufficient for Russia to cause destabilization in Georgia, if necessary. Thus, Moscow prefers that openly pro-Russian parties be represented in the parliament of Georgia only in relatively small factions. But if this is not the case, it will be of little concern to the Kremlin.

For Moscow, it is much more important to maintain a consistently unstable political situation in Georgia in order to hamper the strengthening of its statehood and economic development. As a result, it will be practically impossible for Georgia to access Euro-Atlantic structures, given the persistent instability in the country. Moscow's goal is that notwithstanding the outcomes of the 2020 parliamentary elections in Georgia, they should exacerbate the political situation in the country and lead to an irreconcilable confrontation among the country's political parties.

To achieve this goal, Moscow will use any means available (Knott 2020), including its already traditional cybercrimes (Weinstein, 2019). The most recent cyberattack, which was carried out against Georgia in the fall of 2019 (Browne 2020), can be considered a dress rehearsal to interference with Georgia's upcoming parliamentary elections. The former president of Georgia, Mikheil Saakashvili, can be regarded among the instruments available to the Kremlin for destabilizing the situation in Georgia. He has been successfully used as an instrument for destabilization in Georgia (GT 2015) as well as in Ukraine (Magda 2016).

For Georgia to escape from the political trap set by Moscow and thus avoid further destabilization, it is essential for the government to conduct the 2020 parliamentary elections in a maximally democratic and fair manner without any rigging. The opposition parties should bear in mind that destabilization in Georgia only serves the interests of the Kremlin. In this regard, the agreement reached between the parties with the active participation of some embassies (US, EU, Germany, etc.) on the system for the parliamentary elections of 2020 should be considered encouraging (CG 2020).

References

Berekashvili, B. 2019. "Nationalism and Hegemony in Post-Communist Georgia." *Caucasus Edition. Journal of Conflict Transformation*, March 25, https://caucasusedition.net/

nationalism-and-hegemony-in-post-communist-georgia/ (last accessed March 8, 2020).

Browne, R. 2020. "US and UK Accuse Russia of Major Cyber Attack on Georgia." *CNN*, February 20, https://edition.cnn.com/2020/02/20/politics/russia-georgia-hacking/index.html (last accessed March 8, 2020).

CG. 2019. "Red Cross Visits Georgian Doctor in Tskhinvali Jail." *Civil Georgia*, November 18, https://civil.ge/archives/327860 (last accessed March 8, 2020).

CG. 2020. "Georgian Dream, Opposition Reach Consensus over Electoral Reform." *Civil Georgia*, March 8, https://civil.ge/archives/327860 (last accessed March 8, 2020).

Ellyatt, H. 2019. "Russia is Still Occupying 20% of Our Country, Georgia's Prime Minister Says." *CNBC*, January 22, https://www.cnbc.com/2019/01/22/russia-is-still-occupying-20percent-of-our-country-georgias-leader-says.html (last accessed March 8, 2020).

GJ. 2020. "Bidzina Ivanishvili is Vladimir Putin's Puppet, Says Congressman Olson." *Georgian Journal*, January 29, https://www.georgianjournal.ge/politics/36175-bidzina-ivanishvili-is-vladimir-putins-puppet-says-congressman-olson.html (last accessed March 8, 2020).

GMT. 2004. "Georgian President in Adjaria After Abashidze Flees." *Radio Free Europe/Radio Liberty*, November 22, https://www.rferl.org/a/1052653.html (last accessed March 8, 2020).

GT. 2015. "Gvaramia Confirms Conversation Had with Saakashvili." *Georgia Today*, October 30, http://georgiatoday.ge/news/1741/Gvaramia-Confirms-Conversation-Had-with-Saakashvili (last accessed March 8, 2020).

IPN. 2019. "Nino Burjanadze Insists Georgian Doctor will be Released no Later Than this Friday." *InterPressNews*, December

10, https://www.interpressnews.ge/en/article/104959-nino-burjanadze-insists-georgian-doctor-will-be-released-no-later-than-this-friday/ (last accessed March 8, 2020).

JAMnews. 2019. "Founder of Georgia's Largest Bank Creates Political Party." *JAMnews*, September 13, https://jam-news.net/founder-of-georgias-largest-bank-creates-political-party/ (last accessed March 8, 2020).

Kakachia, K. 2013. "Georgia: Identity, Foreign Policy and the Politics of a 'Euro-Atlantic Orientation.'" *The Norwegian Peacebuilding Resource Centre Policy Brief*, March, https://www.files.ethz.ch/isn/162767/52b05938ffcd3ea8b9c6d499e1515b35.pdf (last accessed March 8, 2020).

Knott, P. 2020. "Putin's Plans to Destabilise Politics Around the World in 2020." *The New European*, January 3, https://www.theneweuropean.co.uk/top-stories/paul-knott-on-vladimir-putin-brexit-and-politics-1-6450371 (last accessed March 8, 2020).

Magda, Y. 2016. "Week's Milestones. Saakashvili Acceleration, Russia's Destabilization Plan for Ukraine, and Complications in Interior Ministry." *UNIAN*, November 14, https://www.unian.info/politics/1623096-weeks-milestones-saakashvili-acceleration-russias-destabilization-plan-for-ukraine-and-complications-in-interior-ministry.html (last accessed March 8, 2020).

Papava, V. 2015. "Economic Models of Eurasianism and the Eurasian Union: Why the Future Is Not Optimistic." *The Central Asia-Caucasus Analyst*, October 29, http://cacianalyst.org/publications/analytical-articles/item/13296 (last accessed March 8, 2020).

Papava, V., and F. Starr. 2006. "Russia's Economic Imperialism." *Project Syndicate*, January 17, http://www.project-syndicate.org/commentary/papava1 (last accessed March 8, 2020).

RFE/RL's Georgian Service. 2019. "Prominent Georgian Doctor Released from Prison in Separatist South Ossetia." *Radio Free Europe/Radio Liberty*, December 28, https://www.rferl.org/a/prominent-georgian-doctor-released-in-separatist-south-ossetia/30348946.html (last accessed March 8, 2020).

Shlamov, V. 2018. "Georgians Vote in Hotly Contested Presidential Runoff." *France 24*, November 28, https://www.france24.com/en/20181128-georgia-second-round-presidential-election-zurabishvili-vashadze (last accessed March 8, 2020).

Sindelar, D. 2008. "Is The Bloom Off The Rose In Georgia?" *Radio Free Europe/Radio Liberty*, November 22, https://www.rferl.org/a/Bloom_Off_Rose_In_Georgia/1351943.html (last accessed March 8, 2020).

Tabula. 2012. "Ivanishvili's Business Interests in Russia: What thou Givest Away is Thine." *Tabula*, July 20, http://www.tabula.ge/en/story/70418-ivanishvilis-business-interests-in-russia-what-thou-givest-away-is-thine (last accessed March 8, 2020).

Traynor, I. 2009. "Georgian President Mikheil Saakashvili Blamed for Starting Russian War." *The Guardian*, September 30, https://www.theguardian.com/world/2009/sep/30/georgia-attacks-unjustifiable-eu (last accessed March 8, 2020).

Weinstein, D. 2019. "We Must Deter Russian Cyberattacks to Prevent a Digital Cold War." *USA Today*, July 6, https://www.usatoday.com/story/opinion/2019/07/06/deter-russian-cyber-attack-cold-war-column/1587711001/ (last accessed March 8, 2020).

Coronic Crisis: When the Economy is a Hostage to Medicine

March 29, 2020[*]

Threats posed by the global spread of the new COVID-19 swept through the modern world, putting substantially new issues on the agenda. Among them is the important issue of how to manage the economy under the circumstances and what changes should be made to reduce future economic risks.

Economists traditionally have been exploring impacts of economic crisis on the overall health care system and on the mental health of the population, as well as on the transmission of communicable diseases. The issue, contrary to the traditional one, is that the coronavirus spurs a large-scale economic crisis

---

[*] V. Papava, "Coronomic Crisis: When the Economy Is a Hostage to Medicine." *Eurasia Review*, March 29, 2020, https://www.eurasiareview.com/29032020-coronomic-crisis-when-the-economy-is-a-hostage-to-medicine-oped/.

and that the coronavirus has actually turned into an "economic pandemic" (Riley 2020).

In order to emphasize the impact of the spread of the coronavirus on the economy, Prof. Ajith de Alwis coined a new term, *coronomics*, which is a merger of the two terms *corona* and *economics*. It studies the negative repercussions of the coronavirus for the economy (de Alwis 2020). Later, a similar term, *coronanomics*, emerged (Eichengreen 2020). The topicality of coronomics is conditioned not only by the fact that the coronavirus is a pandemic but also by the possibility that such threats may occur in the future. This should be taken into consideration both in everyday life in implementing future economic projects.

It is necessary to acknowledge that we face a substantially new type of global economic crisis with causes that, unlike a classic type, are not endogenous but exogenous. That is, these causes are generated outside of the economy and imposed on it by the quick spread of the coronavirus. Given the circumstance, certain countries as well as the whole world are facing a coronomic crisis. It is not yet quite clear how the coronavirus will be overcome or how effective the measures imposed to contain its spread will be. In other words, today, the economy is a hostage to medicine.

Economic difficulties have already affected China and some European countries. With numerous companies closed in the world's second-largest economy and with the developed countries of the EU facing similar difficulties, it is clear that the world is facing threats posed by the coronomic crisis. In fact, the tools (reducing payroll and value-added taxes, increasing social protection, etc.) that are being actively considered are connected to the experience of the global financial and economic crisis of 2008–2009. Whether these measures will be sufficient during this crisis will largely depend on how long it takes the health care industry to develop a treatment for the coronavirus as well as create and produce a relevant vaccine.

It is noteworthy that the above-mentioned measures will ultimately increase the budget deficit and most likely will create a major postcrisis problem in all the countries affected by the pandemic. The fact that the economy is almost idle in China and in a number of European countries will certainly lead to not only decreased demand but also to even more of a decrease in supply (Rogoff 2020). A higher decrease in supply, compared with the decrease in demand, directly affects the increase of inflation. Inflation can be checked by using the tools available for the central banks if they increase interest rates. The latter will further affect supply and economic growth.

This coronomic crisis will probably provide still another argument for economists to prove why inflation targeting does not work anymore, especially for countries that depend on imports (Stiglitz 2008). The spread of the coronavirus has given some boost to ideas against free trade, although it is apparent that those countries that are against globalization will be the ones most affected by the pandemic (Frankel 2020). Taking into consideration that a pandemic is a global phenomenon and the coronomic crisis poses a threat to the whole world, isolationism and deglobalization are clearly disastrous for the world economy. During the postcrisis period, it will be necessary to diversify value and supply chains to ensure the reduction of possible risks.

Thus, special attention should be paid to deconcentrating large companies located in China, which in the future will facilitate reducing those risks which are associated with global threats. Coronomics showed that large companies might find it attractive to relocate their companies in those countries that already have free trade agreements with China (China International Electronic Commerce Center, 2020). In regard to the EU, those countries that have free trade agreements both with the EU and China (such as Iceland, Georgia, and Switzerland) should be highlighted. Among them, a post-Soviet Georgia draws particular attention, as it is located between the EU and China and is a transport corridor linking Europe and Asia (Rzayev and Huseynov 2018).

The interest of the United States in having a free-trade agreement with Georgia should also be taken into consideration (Rapoza 2020). Using Georgia as a regional economic hub can be regarded as one of the strategic directions during the postcrisis development.

References

China International Electronic Commerce Center. 2020. "Cina FTA Network." *Ministry of Commerce, PRC*, http://fta.mofcom.gov.cn/english/fta_qianshu.shtml (last accessed March 25, 2020).

de Alwis, A. 2020. "Coronomics—Plan Your Eggs and the Basket!" *Daily FT*, February 6, http://www.ft.lk/columns/Coronomics-%E2%80%93-Plan-your-eggs-and-the-basket-/4-695109 (last accessed March 25, 2020).

Eichengreen B. 2020. "Coronanomics 101." *Project Syndicate*, March 10, https://www.project-syndicate.org/commentary/limits-macroeconomic-tools-coronavirus-pandemic-by-barry-eichengreen-2020-03?utm_source=Project%20Syndicate%20Newsletter&utm_campaign=cba7e1c6a1-sunday_newsletter_15_03_2020&utm_medium=email&utm_term=0_73bad5b7d8-cba7e1c6a1-93567601&mc_cid=cba7e1c6a1&mc_eid=e9fb6cbcc0&barrier=accesspaylog (last accessed March 25, 2020).

Frankel, J. 2020. "Will the Coronavirus Trigger a Global Recession?" *Project Syndicate*, 2020, February 24, https://www.project-syndicate.org/commentary/coronavirus-global-recession-prospects-by-jeffrey-frankel-2020-02?utm_source=Project%20Syndicate%20Newsletter&utm_campaign=11fa1362d7-sunday_newsletter_01_03_2020&utm_medium=email&utm_term=0_73bad5b7d8-11fa1362d7-93567601&mc_cid=11fa1362d7&mc_eid=e9fb6cbcc0&barrier=accesspaylog (last accessed March 25, 2020).

Riley, C. 2020. "Coronavirus is Fast Becoming an 'Economic Pandemic'." *CNN*, February 25, https://edition.cnn.com/2020/02/20/politics/russia-georgia-hacking/index.html (last accessed March 25, 2020).

Rogoff, K. 2020. "That 1970s Feeling." *Project Syndicate*, 2020, March 2, https://www.project-syndicate.org/commentary/next-global-recession-hits-the-supply-side-by-kenneth-rogoff-2020-03?utm_source=Project%20Syndicate%20Newsletter&utm_campaign=5a74e31e27-sunday_newsletter_08_03_

2020&utm_medium=email&utm_term=0_73bad5b7d8-5a74e31e27-93567601&mc_cid=5a74e31e27&mc_eid=e9fb6cbcc0&barrier=accesspaylog (last accessed March 25, 2020).

Rapoza, K. 2020. "Why Does Everyone Suddenly Want A Free Trade Deal With Georgia?" *Forbes*, March 5, https://www.forbes.com/sites/kenrapoza/2020/03/05/why-does-everyone-suddenly-want-a-free-trade-deal-with-georgia/#121c381350e6 (last accessed March 25, 2020).

Rzayev, A., and V. Huseynov. 2018. "South Caucasus Eyes Becoming a Hub Along EU–China Transportation Route." *The Jamestown Foundation, Eurasia Daily Monitor*, Vol. 15, Iss. 158, November 6, https://jamestown.org/program/south-caucasus-eyes-becoming-a-hub-along-eu-china-transportation-route/ (last accessed March 25, 2020).

Stiglitz, J. E. 2008. "The Failure of Inflation Targeting." *Project Syndicate*, May 6, https://www.project-syndicate.org/commentary/the-failure-of-inflation-targeting?barrier=accesspaylog (last accessed March 25, 2020).

34

Pensions, Economic Growth, Agflation, and Inflation

May 13, 2020*

The year 2020 will be marked in world history by the coronavirus pandemic and the global economic crisis it sparked. A new term, *coronomics* (de Alwis 2020), has been coined in order to underline the economic difficulties generated by the coronavirus pandemic. It was precisely this coronomic crisis (Papava 2020) that has gripped most of the states around the world, with leaders being forced to formulate and implement anti-crisis measures (IMF 2020a) in order to ease the social situation for their populations as well as reduce the potential losses to their economies.

At the end of April 2020, the government of Georgia presented its anti-crisis plan (CG 2020), stating that "pensions

---

* V. Papava, "Pensions, Economic Growth, Agflation and Inflation." *Rondeli Blog*, May 13, 2020, https://www.gfsis.org/blog/view/1071.

will rise annually at a rate no less than that of inflation." The plan also specified (AG 2020) that an increase in pensions for people above the age of seventy years will be adjusted based on 80 percent of economic growth as well as the inflation rate. Despite the fact that this issue has already been analyzed (Kvaratskhelia 2019) in a rather detailed manner, there remain several points that require clarification.

The idea of pensions being linked with the economic growth of the country is, at a glance, not at all problematic for economists given the fact that a growing economy, *ceteris paribus*, generates more revenues and sets a noninflationary basis for increasing the amounts of pensions. However, if economic growth is negative, which is to say if a recession takes place, tying pensions to economic growth must logically mean their reduction. If we also take into account that given the forecasts made by the International Monetary Fund (IMF 2020b) the coronomic crisis will cause an economic recession in the absolute majority of states around the world, connecting pensions to economic growth, especially during the coronomic crisis, cannot be justified as a matter of principle.

Irrespective of whether or not the economic growth rate is positive or negative, the reduction of pension payments is unacceptable. As for the indexation of pensions with regard to growing inflation—which means that the growth of pensions must not fall behind the growth of the inflation rate (Lake 2019)—this in itself requires familiarity with certain issues. Taking into account that inflation reduces the purchasing power of pensions, it is obligatory to analyze how beneficial the indexation of pensions or retirement incomes with regard to inflation will be for pensioners.

As of March 2020, the amount of old-age pension in Georgia exceeded the subsistence minimum of a working-age male only slightly: 1.07 times. Given such a situation, the lion's share of a pension is spent on essential products, especially food. Due to this, the growth of pensions causes the growth of the demand on essential products, especially food—which, other conditions being equal, will have an influence on the growth of the prices of these products.

Economists refer to agricultural inflation, or the growth of the average prices of agricultural products, as *agflation* (McMahon 2011). This indicator is usually highly noted in developing as well as developed states (Charaia and Papava 2018). The growth of the average price of essential products (nutrition, utilities, and medication) is called *munflation* (Charaia and Papava 2017).

Given the fact that pensions in Georgia are only slightly higher than the subsistence minimum, the growth of pensions will directly lead to the growth of agflation. The special importance of the latter is also confirmed by official statistics (NSOG 2020b) as, during the coronomic crisis, the level of agflation in Georgia grew faster than the level of inflation. More specifically, in April 2020, the price of fruit grew by 45 percent, of dairy products by 23 percent, of meat products by 15 percent, and of bread products by 8.4 percent, while the annual level of inflation grew by just 6.9 percent as compared to the same period last year. As for munflation, the components that reflect the growth of prices on utilities and medication/treatment are less susceptible to change during the coronomic crisis, which is mostly due to the special support of the government vis-à-vis these fields.

If we consider all this logically, the growth of pensions in accordance with the growth of inflation will directly affect the growth of the rate of agflation, which will ultimately cause the inflation rate to go up. Here, we naturally have a question about how much the growth of the level of agflation will affect the growth of inflation in Georgia. In order to answer this question, one must necessarily take into account the share of the food basket in the overall consumer basket, as the former is used in calculating agflation, while the latter is essential for determining the inflation rate.

According to the official methodology of Georgia for calculating inflation (NSOG 2020a), the share of food products in the consumer basket is just 28 percent. It is worth noting that the share of food products in the consumer basket in post-Communist states that are more or less similar to Georgia in terms of their economic situation is much higher (EPRC 2012). Namely, it is 1.8 times higher in Azerbaijan, Russia, and Armenia, double in Tajikistan, and 2.1 times higher in Uzbekistan.

It is a fact that the share of food products in the consumer basket has been artificially reduced in Georgia. Therefore, the influence of agflation on the growth of inflation is also artificially reduced. Such a situation leads us to the following conclusions:

- Tying the amount of pensions to the level of inflation cannot guarantee that the growing level of agflation caused by the growth of pensions will actually be compensated.
- The indexation of the pension in accordance with the growth level of inflation cannot have a serious influence on the level of inflation itself.

Hence, the growth of the amount of pensions in accordance with the growth of the level of inflation will not significantly improve the quality of life of pensioners, nor will it have any serious effect on the growth of the inflation rate.

At the same time, the indexation of pensions in accordance with the level of inflation will create the undesired precedent of not only indexing pensions but also putting the indexing of wages with regard to inflation on the agenda. This will doubtless put the economy of our country in the inflationary spiral so familiar to economists.

The mechanism of the inflationary spiral is rather simple. The growth of wages in accordance with inflation causes the growth of demand, which makes the prices of products and services in the consumer basket increase. Given the fact that inflation is calculated precisely on the basis of the growth of the average prices of products and services in the consumer basket, the growing price of the consumer basket means that the level of inflation will also rise—which, in the case of the indexation of wages with regard to inflation, also requires wages to increase. The latter causes the level of inflation to increase, which will again require the growth of wages and so forth. Consequently, as we have already stated, the indexation of the amounts of pensions in Georgia will fail to ease the social situation of pensioners while increasing the threat that the country will be dragged into an inflationary spiral.

In conclusion, it is necessary to say that we consider formally tying the amounts of pensions to economic growth to be unjustified, and especially so when pensions are tied to the level of inflation. The pension policy must be complex and flexible. The growth of the amounts of pensions will always be a priority for the government, and every decision will take all economic factors (including the levels of economic growth and inflation) into account in a complex manner.

References

AG. 2020. "Georgia Intends to Index Pensions Based on Inflation, Economic Growth." *Agenda Georgia*, April 28, https://agenda.ge/en/news/2020/1325 (last accessed May 10, 2020).

CG. 2020. "Prime Minister Gakharia Unveils Anti-Crisis Plan to Mitigate Coronavirus Fallout." *Civil Georgia*, April 24, https://civil.ge/archives/348469 (last accessed May 10, 2020).

Charaia, V., and V. Papava. 2017. "From Inflation to Imflation, Agflation and Munflation." *The Market Oracle*, April 6, http://www.marketoracle.co.uk/Article58686.html (last accessed May 10, 2020).

Charaia, V., and V. Papava. 2018. "Agflation and Other Modifications of Inflation (the Cases of Georgia and Its Neighboring Countries)." *Annals of Agrarian Science*, Vol. 16, Iss. 2, https://www.sciencedirect.com/science/article/pii/

S1512188718300897?via%3Dihub (last accessed May 10, 2020).

de Alwis A. 2020. "Coronomics—Plan Your Eggs and the Basket!" *Daily FT*, February 6, http://www.ft.lk/columns/Coronomics-%E2%80%93-Plan-your-eggs-and-the-basket-/4-695109 (last accessed May 10, 2020).

EPRC. 2012. "Inflation in Georgia—Causes and Cures." *Economic Policy Research Center Issue in Focus*, 5th Report, June, https://csogeorgia.org/storage/app/uploads/public/5cd/c9b/3d8/5cdc9b3d8940b313379272.pdf (last accessed May 10, 2020).

IMF. 2020a. "Policy Responses to COVID-19." *International Monetary Fund*, May 8, https://www.imf.org/en/Topics/imf-and-covid19/Policy-Responses-to-COVID-19#U (last accessed May 10, 2020).

IMF. 2020b. "World Economic Outlook, April 2020: The Great Lockdown." *International Monetary Fund*, April, https://www.imf.org/en/Publications/WEO/Issues/2020/04/14/weo-april-2020 (last accessed May 10, 2020).

Kvaratskhelia, V. 2019. "If the Government of Georgia decides to index pensions, possible annual growth of pensions will be GEL 8-11 only." *Factcheck.ge*, January 18, https://factcheck.ge/en/story/37924-if-the-government-of-georgia-decides-to-index-pensions-possible-annual-growth-of-pensions-will-be-gel-8-11-only (last accessed May 10, 2020).

Lake, R. 2019. "How Inflation Eats Away at Your Retirement Income." *Investopedia*, November 21, https://www.investopedia.com/articles/retirement/052616/how-inflation-eats-away-your-retirement.asp (last accessed May 10, 2020).

McMahon, T. 2011. "Agflation—What is it?" *InflationData.com*, February 16, https://inflationdata.com/articles/2011/02/16/agflation-what-is-it/ (last accessed May 10, 2020).

NSOG. 2020a. "Inflation Calculation Methodology Note." *National Statistics Office of Georgia*, https://www.geostat.ge/media/29192/Inflation-calculation-methodology-note_2020.pdf (last accessed May 10, 2020).

NSOG. 2020b. "Inflation Rate In Georgia, April 2020." *National Statistics Office of Georgia*, May 4, https://www.geostat.ge/media/31099/Inflation-Rate-in-Georgia---april---2020.pdf (last accessed May 10, 2020).

Papava, V. 2020. "Coronomic Crisis: When the Economy Is a Hostage to Medicine." *Eurasia Review*, March 29, https://www.eurasiareview.com/29032020-coronomic-crisis-when-the-economy-is-a-hostage-to-medicine-oped/ (last accessed May 10, 2020).

35

Georgia's European Way During the Period of Pandemic Deglobalization

August 6, 2020[*]

The COVID-19 pandemic has had a significant influence on both the lives of individuals and the world economy, requiring the reconsideration of a number of issues. Among them, the problem of globalization deserves special attention. In particular, will the COVID-19 pandemic lead to the end of globalization as such, and will deglobalization utterly and permanently replace globalization, leading to isolationism?

Despite warnings from experts about the impending danger of a flu pandemic, unfortunately, this was not taken into account (Rodrik 2020b) and led to the extensive spreading

---

[*] V. Papava, "Georgia's European Way During the Period of Pandemic Deglobalization," *Rondeli Blog*, August 6, 2020, https://www.gfsis.org/blog/view/1091.

of COVID-19. In turn, the COVID-19 pandemic has well illustrated the weaknesses of modern globalization: the rapid spread of the virus has shown to everyone that global institutions and, above all, the World Health Organization do not actually possess effective mechanisms for a quick response. As a result, each state began to act independently against the pandemic, creating and reinforcing a sense that we are dealing with a process of deglobalization.

The COVID-19 pandemic was perceived by many as a globalization crisis. Therefore, it is logical to ask: Is the process of deglobalization really possible or not? And if it is possible, then to what extent is it desirable?

First of all, it should be noted that globalization is an objective process. The most obvious example of this is the illegal drug business, which is fought against by both individual states and international organizations but nevertheless is a business that has long taken on a global character. No less important in the context of globalization are the Internet, energy, the arms trade, the expansion of the US dollar, and so on. And today, the spread of COVID-19 has become a serious global problem.

Of course, deglobalization is quite possible. To do this, a country must consciously pursue a more or less isolationist policy, although it should be borne in mind that this will have a negative impact not only on economic growth (Rogoff 2020) but also on social, political, and environmental issues (Haass 2020). Thus, deglobalization will ultimately further complicate the resolution of those problems that plague mankind. In my opinion, in the modern world, there is mainly a so-called forced deglobalization, precipitated by the fact that the mass spread of COVID-19 was sudden and rapid. No one was prepared to act against this problem, so all states acted more or less in isolation.

But because of the global nature of the problem itself, overcoming a pandemic in isolationism is simply unthinkable. Coordinated action on a global scale is essential (Mazzucato and Torreele 2020). Moreover, countries that oppose free trade will be more damaged economically (Åslund 2020). Only by promoting free trade will countries be able to more or less successfully use their comparative advantage to alleviate the consequences of the economic crisis (Fung 2020) caused by the pandemic.

At the same time, it is certainly noteworthy that the process of deglobalization, which was initiated by US President Donald Trump even before COVID-19 (Sachs 2017) and deepened in the conditions of the pandemic, is likely to be more or less trendy for some time. In this situation, it is necessary for countries to prepare as much as possible to move to a qualitatively higher level of renewed globalization (El-Erian 2020). Moreover, it would be a mistake if countries do not pay attention to the realities of deglobalization; that is, the role of the government in the economy becoming stronger as the national autonomy deepens (Rodrik 2020a).

It is precisely in the context of deglobalization that the novel resolution of a number of problems is to be conceived, such as food security (Blair and Kalibata 2020). The severity of this problem is underscored by Russia's decision to suspend wheat exports (Medetsky and Durisin 2020) in order to ensure its own food security. In turn, the reduction of the wheat supply to international markets will lead to an increase in prices, and this will have a severe impact on countries for which the import of Russian wheat is of great importance. Georgia is one of these countries.

Therefore, it is necessary for Georgia to take into account the peculiarities of modern deglobalization. For example, in Georgia, which has favorable natural climatic conditions for agricultural production and where almost half of the able-bodied population lives in rural areas, the share of the agricultural sector in the GDP is less than 8 percent, and the country's industrial sector is unfortunately underdeveloped. One of the priority issues for Georgia is to address food security by promoting the development of local agricultural production.

In terms of Georgia's economic development, Georgia is the only country in the region that has free trade regimes with both the EU and China, which is and will be of particular importance for the diversification of value chains and supply chains (Derviş and Strauss 2020) in the pandemic and postpandemic periods. In this context, it should be noted that it is quite real for Georgia to have a free trade regime with the United States (Rapoza 2020) as well, which will open up new perspectives for the development of the Georgian economy.

It is especially important to understand how Georgia's European choice (Papava 2017) should be viewed in the postpandemic period. First of all, the question must be answered: Is EU membership a goal for Georgia or a means to an end? And if it is a means to an end, then what should the goal be?

It is my deepest belief that membership in any union cannot be the goal, as it must be seen as a means to a larger end. In particular, Georgia aims to be a European state. For that to happen, everyone, both Georgian citizens and foreigners, must be fully convinced that Georgia has become a truly European state. The fact that, for example, Switzerland or Iceland are not members of the European Union does not necessarily mean that anyone can doubt the Europeanness of these states. This is precisely the situation Georgia should achieve.

For this purpose, it is necessary to establish the standards emblematic of a European state in Georgia. This is possible by adopting democratic traditions, human rights, freedom of speech and expression, a European-style market economy, and a public administration system currently practiced in the EU countries into the Georgian reality. In order for Georgia to become a European state, it must carry out the appropriate reforms for EU membership. The route to joining the European Union is the way to establish Georgia as a European state. And in this situation, the question of whether or not Georgia will eventually join the EU will become mainly technical in nature and greatly depend on the stage of development of the EU itself.

The fact is that the European Union is in a very difficult situation today because the COVID-19 pandemic was added to the damage caused by Brexit, which the EU met unprepared (Varoufakis 2020). At the same time, the COVID-19 pandemic posed a serious challenge to the EU, establishing that a strong crisis management mechanism is necessary (Reichlin 2020). In this context, the decision of the European Union regarding the seven-year budget and the elimination of the damage caused by the coronavirus (Herszenhorn and Bayer 2020) should indeed be assessed as optimistic. In the current context of EU-Georgia relations, it is particularly noteworthy that as a result of Georgia's success in overcoming the COVID-19 epidemic, Georgia has been among the fifteen countries with which the EU has decided to open its borders (EU 2020).

In addition to Georgia's goal of becoming a European-type country, it is no less important to maintain state independence in order to minimize threats from Russia. In this sense, EU membership can also be seen as an effective way to maintain independence from Russia. As is well known, a particularly strong mechanism for maintaining independence from Russia is NATO membership, despite the fact that due to the difficulties in relations between its member states, NATO itself has faced quite difficult challenges (Palacio 2020).

Given the current situation, Georgia should make the most of all opportunities to become a European state independent from Russia. The possibility of this is not ruled out by the current trend of pandemic deglobalization.

References

Åslund, A. 2020. "Trump's Global Recession." *Project Syndicate*, March 13, https://www.project-syndicate.org/commentary/donald-trump-covid19-global-recession-by-anders-aslund-2020-03?barrier=accesspaylog (last accessed August 3, 2020).

Blair, T., and A. Kalibata. 2020. "Building Food Security During the Pandemic." *Project Syndicate*, May 7, https://www.project-syndicate.org/commentary/four-ways-to-boost-food-security-during-covid19-pandemic-by-tony-blair-and-agnes-kalibata-2020-05?utm_source=Project%20Syndicate%20Newsletter&utm_campaign=2ad6876daf-sunday_newsletter_10_05_2020&utm_medium=email&utm_term=0_73bad5b7d8-2ad6876daf-93567601&mc_cid=2ad6876daf&mc_eid=e9fb6cbcc0&barrier=accesspaylog (last accessed August 3, 2020).

Derviş, K., and S. Strauss. 2020. "What COVID-19 Means for International Cooperation." *Project Syndicate*, March 6, https://www.project-syndicate.org/commentary/global-cooperation-can-prevent-next-pandemic-by-kemal-dervis-and-sebasti-n-strauss-2020-03?utm_source=Project%20Syndicate%20Newsletter&utm_campaign=cba7e1c6a1-sunday_newsletter_15_03_2020&utm_medium=email&utm_term=0_73bad5b7d8-cba7e1c6a1-93567601&mc_cid=cba7e1c6a1&mc_eid=e9fb6cbcc0&barrier=accesspaylog (last accessed August 3, 2020).

El-Erian, M. A. 2020. "Navigating Deglobalization." *Project Syndicate*, May 11, https://www.project-syndicate.org/commentary/covid19-deglobalization-two-priorities-by-mohamed-a-el-erian-2020-05?utm_source=Project%20Syndicate%20Newsletter&utm_campaign=3ce69c95d3-sunday_

newsletter_17_05_2020&utm_medium=email&utm_term=0_73bad5b7d8-3ce69c95d3-93567601&mc_cid=3ce69c95d3&mc_eid=e9fb6cbcc0&barrier=accesspaylog (last accessed August 3, 2020).

EU. 2020. "Georgia Among First 15 Countries to Which EU will Reopen Its Borders on 1st July." *Delegation of the European Union to Georgia*, June 30, https://eeas.europa.eu/delegations/georgia/81824/georgia-among-first-15-countries-which-eu-will-reopen-its-borders-1st-july_en (last accessed August 3, 2020).

Fung, V. K. 2020. "The Trade Cure for the Global Economy." *Project Syndicate*, April 22, https://www.project-syndicate.org/commentary/covid19-crisis-revive-multilateralism-open-trade-by-victor-k-fung-2020-04?utm_source=Project%20Syndicate%20Newsletter&utm_campaign=871db40e9f-sunday_newsletter_26_04_2020&utm_medium=email&utm_term=0_73bad5b7d8-871db40e9f-93567601&mc_cid=871db40e9f&mc_eid=e9fb6cbcc0&barrier=accesspaylog (last accessed August 3, 2020).

Haass, R. N. 2020. "Deglobalization and Its Discontents." *Project Syndicate*, May 12, https://www.project-syndicate.org/commentary/deglobalizaton-discontents-by-richard-n-haass-2020-05?utm_source=Project%20Syndicate%20Newsletter&utm_campaign=3ce69c95d3-sunday_newsletter_17_05_2020&utm_medium=email&utm_term=0_73bad5b7d8-3ce69c95d3-93567601&mc_cid=3ce69c95d3&mc_eid=e9fb6cbcc0&barrier=accesspaylog (last accessed August 3, 2020).

Herszenhorn, D. M., and L. Bayer. 2020. "EU Leaders Agree on €1.82T Budget and Coronavirus Recovery Package." *Politico*, July 20, https://www.politico.eu/article/eu-leaders-reach-deal-on-coronavirus-recovery-fund/ (last accessed August 3, 2020).

Mazzucato, M., and E. Torreele. 2020. "How to Develop a COVID-19 Vaccine for All." *Project Syndicate*, April 27, https://www.project-syndicate.org/commentary/universal-free-covid19-vaccine-by-mariana-mazzucato-and-els-torreele-2020-04?utm_source=Project%20Syndicate%20Newsletter&utm_campaign=64d8372856-sunday_newsletter_03_05_2020&utm_medium=email&utm_term=0_73bad5b7d8-64d8372856-93567601&mc_cid=64d8372856&mc_eid=e9fb6cbcc0&barrier=accesspaylog (last accessed August 3, 2020).

Medetsky, A., and M. Durisin. 2020. "Russia Halts Wheat Exports, Deepening Fears of Global Food Shortages." *Time*, April 27, https://time.com/5827804/russia-wheat-food-shortage/ (last accessed August 3, 2020).

Palacio, A. 2020. "NATO Is Dying." *Project Syndicate*, July 15, https://www.project-syndicate.org/commentary/france-turkey-naval-row-nato-by-ana-palacio-2020-07?utm_source=Project+Syndicate+Newsletter&utm_campaign=6a78f0e5f0-sunday_newsletter_19_07_2020&utm_medium=email&utm_term=0_73bad5b7d8-6a78f0e5f0-93567601&mc_cid=6a78f0e5f0&mc_eid=e9fb6cbcc0 (last accessed August 3, 2020).

Papava, V. 2017. "For Georgia GEENTRANCE Is Coming!" *Eurasia Review*, January 5, https://www.eurasiareview.com/05012017-for-georgia-geentrance-is-coming-oped/ (last accessed August 3, 2020).

Rapoza, K. 2020. "Why Does Everyone Suddenly Want A Free Trade Deal With Georgia?" *Forbes*, March 5, https://www.forbes.com/sites/kenrapoza/2020/03/05/why-does-everyone-suddenly-want-a-free-trade-deal-with-georgia/#2f0187dc50e6 (last accessed August 3, 2020).

Reichlin, L. 2020. "COVID-19 Is an Opportunity for Europe." *Project Syndicate*, March 10, https://www.project-syndicate.org/commentary/eu-covid19-response-coordinated-fiscal-stimulus-by-lucrezia-reichlin-2020-03?utm_source=Project%20Syndicate%20Newsletter&utm_campaign=cba7e1c6a1-sunday_newsletter_15_03_2020&utm_medium=email&utm_term=0_73bad5b7d8-cba7e1c6a1-93567601&mc_cid=cba7e1c6a1&mc_eid=e9fb6cbcc0&barrier=accesspaylog (last accessed August 3, 2020).

Rodrik, D. 2020a. "Making the Best of a Post-Pandemic World." *Project Syndicate*, May 12, https://www.project-syndicate.org/commentary/three-trends-shaping-post-pandemic-global-economy-by-dani-rodrik-2020-05?utm_source=Project%20Syndicate%20Newsletter&utm_campaign=3ce69c95d3-sunday_newsletter_17_05_2020&utm_medium=email&utm_term=0_73bad5b7d8-3ce69c95d3-93567601&mc_cid=3ce69c95d3&mc_eid=e9fb6cbcc0&barrier=accesspaylog (last accessed August 3, 2020).

Rodrik, D. 2020b. "Will COVID-19 Remake the World?" *Project Syndicate*, April 6, https://www.project-syndicate.org/commentary/will-covid19-remake-the-world-by-dani-rodrik-2020-04?utm_source=Project%20Syndicate%20Newsletter&utm_campaign=aa811cf03a-covid_newsletter_09_04_2020&utm_medium=email&utm_term=0_73bad5b7d8-aa811cf03a-93567601&mc_cid=aa811cf03a&mc_eid=e9fb6cbcc0&barrier=accesspaylog (last accessed August 3, 2020).

Rogoff, K. 2020. "Deglobalization will Hurt Growth Everywhere." *Project Syndicate*, June 3, https://www.project-syndicate.org/commentary/deglobalization-threat-to-world-economy-and-united-states-by-kenneth-rogoff-2020-06?utm_ source=Project%20Syndicate%20Newsletter&utm_campaign=56f4462bc8-sunday_newsletter_07_06_2020&utm_medium=email&utm_term=0_73bad5b7d8-56f4462bc8-93567601&mc_cid=56f4462bc8&mc_eid=e9fb6cbcc0&barrier=accesspaylog (last accessed August 3, 2020).

Sachs, J. 2017. "Global Cooperation is the Only Way Forward for the US." *World Economic Forum*, January 6, https://www.weforum.org/agenda/2017/01/jeffrey-sachs-global-cooperation-is-the-only-way-forward-for-the-us/ (last accessed August 3, 2020).

Varoufakis, Y. 2020. "Europe Is Unprepared for the COVID-19 Recession." *Project Syndicate*, March 18, https://www.project-syndicate.org/commentary/eurogroup-finance-ministers-misunderstand-covid19-crisis-by-yanis-varoufakis-2020-03?utm_source=Project%20Syndicate%20Newsletter&utm_campaign=fc0dee22cd-sunday_newsletter_22_03_2020&utm_medium=email&utm_term=0_73bad5b7d8-fc0dee22cd-93567601&mc_cid=fc0dee22cd&mc_eid=e9fb6cbcc0&barrier=accesspaylog (last accessed August 3, 2020).

INDEX

A

Abashidze, Aslan, 75, 128
Abashidze, Giorgi, 128
Abkhazia
    as secessionist Georgian province, 4
    annexation of by Russia, xviii, 20
    border monitors in, 113–114, 115–116
    independence of, 11
    Russia as recognizing independence of, 49, 50, 51, 59, 60, 61, 95, 110, 112, 127
    Russian citizenship as granted to residents of, 7, 33, 34, 50, 60
    Russian military bases in, 49, 51, 95
    Russian troops in, 7
AES Silk Road, 2
Agency for Financial Supervision, 67
agricultural inflation (agflation), 143, 248, 249, 250
agriculture sector, 143, 147, 257
Ahmadinejad, Mahmoud, 4
Ajara
    Autonomous Republic of, 75
    budgeting process in, 12–13
    control of by local strongman, 11
    revolution, 128, 233
Alasania, Irakli, 95
Alliance of Patriots of Georgia (APG), 233

alternative pipelines
paradigm, 24
Amaghlobeli, David, 39
Anaklia Black Sea Deep Water
Port, 195
antimonopoly regulation
abolishment of, 15, 68,
104, 107, 139, 154
need for, 44, 47, 69, 94,
95, 107, 108, 140,
145, 148, 155
Arab Spring, 120
Armed Forces of Georgia,
14, 125
Armenia
and Free Economic Zone
(FEZ), 161
and Gazprom, 3, 6, 129,
175–176
and Georgia, 116, 129,
146, 149
and Russia, 4, 116, 129,
146, 155
and Turkey, 115, 116
as EAEU member, 157,
159, 161, 165,
169, 231
as part of Central Eurasia,
27, 28
as part of the Caucasus, 29
consumer basket, 249

corruption in, 166
debt to Russia, 2
GDP of, 153
market reforms in, 159
plans for rail link to Iran
with Russia, 4
price of gas in (November
2016), 175,
176, 177
Russian ownership of
gas pipelines and
railways in, 174
Russia's interest in seeing
pro-Russian
political parties
come to power
in, 231
Armenian-Azerbaijani
conflict 175
Armenian Railways, 174
Armsberbank, 3
ASEAN, 160
Azerbaijan
and purchase of Georgian
assets, 175
as one of Georgia's
main trading
partners, 204
as part of Central Eurasia,
27, 28

as part of Central Eurasia, 27, 28
as part of the Caucasus, 29
consumer basket, 249
economic growth of, 153
gas supplies from, 8
inclusion of in SREB project, 191, 192
Azerbaijani railways, 174

B

Bakhtadze, Mamuka, 199, 219
Baku-Tbilisi-Ceyhan (BTC), 24
Baku-Tbilisi-Kars railway, 195
Baku-Tbilisi-Supsa (BTS), 24
Balcerowicz, Lesek, 226
Balcerowicz Plan, 226
bank loans, 197, 198. *See also* consumer loans
banking sector, 38, 42, 43, 142, 206
Beeline, 130
Beijing, Belt and Road Initiative (BRI), 191–195
Belarus
    corruption in, 170
    economy of, 159
    as founding member of EAEU, 157, 159, 160, 165, 169
    and Free Economic Zone (FEZ), 161
    Russia's interest in seeing pro-Russian political parties come to power in, 231
    Russia's pressure on, 23–24
Belt and Road Initiative (BRI), 191–195
Ben Ali, 119, 120
Bendukidze, Kakha, 129, 130, 152, 154, 211, 226
Biltmore Tbilisi, 189
Black Sea Synergy, 106
border monitors, 113
BRI (Belt and Road Initiative), 191–195
BTC (Baku-Tbilisi-Ceyhan), 24
BTS (Baku-Tbilisi-Supsa), 24
budget manipulations, 72–73
budgetary crisis, 12, 87, 139
Bulgaria, 25, 26, 147
    corruption in, 166, 170
Burgas-Alexandropolis, 25
Burjanadze, Nino, 95, 234–235

Bush, George W., 20, 134
business administration, public administration as compared to, 212
business start-ups, registration for, 139, 145, 152, 226

C

Caspian Basin states, as source of energy resources for EU, 24
The Caucasus, use of term, 28–29
CEA (Council of Economic Advisors), 213
Central Asia, use of term, 28, 30
Central Asia–West Asia Economic Corridor, 191, 192
Central Caucaso-Asia, use of term, 30
Central Caucasus, 29
Central Eurasia, use of term, 27
Chechnya, 58
China
    free-trade regime of with EU, 194
    impacts of COVID-19 in, 241, 242, 243
    investment of in Georgia, 195
    model of economic modernization of, 193
Chubais, Anatoli, 1, 2, 3, 91
civil servant force, changes in, 15
Clear City, 71
Clinton, Hillary, 135
Cold War, new threats of, 56–63
command economy, 139, 187, 225
Commonwealth of Independent States (CIS), xvii, 50, 171, 172
competition, limitation of, 68–69
constitution
    changes to, 11–12, 122, 184
    disrespect for, 17, 90
consumer borrowing, 142
consumer loans, 198. *See also* bank loans
consumer rights protection, 44, 47, 94, 95, 140, 145, 148
consumerism, 144, 197, 198
coronanomics, 241
coronavirus. *See* COVID-19

coronomics, 241–243, 246
corruption, 10, 13, 16, 18, 67, 87, 88, 89, 90–91, 104–106, 139–140, 151, 156, 166, 171
Corruption Perceptions Index study, 166, 170
Council of Economic Advisors (CEA), 213
Council of Europe, 11
COVID-19, impacts of, xviii, 240–243, 246–251, 254–259
cryptocurrencies, 225
currency reform, 139
currency reserves, 46, 78, 206
customs monitoring, 114
cybercrimes, 236
Cyprus, as model of development for Georgia, 51, 53–54, 165

D

De Alwis, Ajith, 241
Deep and Comprehensive Free Trade Area (DCFTA), xviii, 107, 108, 155, 164, 170, 180, 185, 194, 195
deglobalization, 243, 254, 255–256, 257, 259

Department of Wine Export, establishment of, 155
deprivatization, 17, 65, 90, 105–106
deregulation, 88
development, models of, 49–55, 140–144
Doing Business (World Bank), 17, 89, 103, 104, 153

E

EAEU (Eurasian Economic Union). *See* Eurasian Economic Union (EAEU)
Eastern Partnership (EaP), 54, 106, 108, 170
economic model(s)
　comparisons of, 108, 158, 159, 162
　in Georgia, 140, 181, 186, 196–201, 217
"economic pandemic," 241
economic policy
　as often in conflict with basic economic tenets, 222
　noneconomic policy, 222–227
　primitivism of Georgia's, 179–186

269

economic program, 71, 83–84
economic reforms, 14, 102–108, 138–140, 152, 156, 181, 226
economists, need for in Georgia, 187, 202, 209–214
EFTA (European Free Trade Association), 160, 194
EGML (European Georgia Movement for Liberty), 232, 233
elections
    parliamentary elections (2008), 83
    parliamentary elections (2012), 121, 132, 144, 189, 214
    parliamentary elections (2016), 163, 173, 181
    parliamentary elections (2020), 233, 235, 236
    rigging of, 95
elections cycle, 80
electric-car factory, 220
elites, corruption among, 18, 90, 105, 139
emigration, 142

employer-employee relations, 73–75
Energo-Pro, 67
energy crisis, 10, 87, 88, 139
energy sector
    combat of corruption in, 88
    corruption in, 13
ENP (European Neighborhood Policy), 44, 94, 106, 170
Eskene-Kurik oil pipeline, 25
Ethnic Georgians, as targets of persecution in Russia, 7, 60
EU-Georgia Association Agreement (AA), xviii, 155, 164, 168, 169, 180, 185
Eurasian Economic Union (EAEU), 157, 159, 160, 161, 162, 165, 166, 168, 169, 172, 177, 192, 193, 194, 231
Eurasian Union, economic models of, 157–162
Eurasianism, economic models of, 157–162
Eurasianism Doctrine, 158
Eurobonds, 79–80

Europe, as fostering South Caucasus's links with West, 4
European Free Trade Association (EFTA), 160, 194
European Georgia Movement for Liberty (EGML), 232, 233
European Neighborhood Policy (ENP), 44, 94, 106, 170
European Union
    and Brexit, xviii, 166, 259
    as contrasted with EAEU, 169–171
    COVID-19 and, 259
    Georgia's ambition to join, 106, 164, 168, 257–258
    initial purpose of, 169
    problems of, 166
    reasons for success of, 172
    standards for membership in, 170–171
excise tax, 184
exports, composition of, 141
extrabudgetary accounts, 16, 88, 89–90, 105, 153

F

FDI (foreign direct investments), 44, 93, 141, 142, 199
FEZ (Free Economic Zone), 75–76, 160–161
financial pyramid scheme, 141
Financial Supervision Agency, 78
Finland, as model of development for Georgia, 51–52
Fitoussi, Jean-Paul, 217
food products, share of in consumer basket, 143, 183, 249
food security, 256–257
food-safety regulations, 107, 108, 140, 155
foreign debt, 73, 79–80
foreign direct investments (FDI), 44, 93, 141, 142, 199
four-point plan, 181–185, 212, 227
fourth zone, establishment of, 159
France, and tourism, 200
Free Economic Zone (FEZ), 75–76, 160–161

free trade agreement (FTA), 140, 144, 145, 146, 148, 149, 194, 195, 204–205, 243

freedom of press, curtailment of, 15

freedom of speech, 121, 133, 170, 258

free-trade regime, 42, 44, 47, 48, 54, 69, 94, 107, 108, 140, 146, 148, 194, 256, 257

Future Generations and Stable Development Funds, 79–80

G

G-8, changing G-7 format to, 58

Gaddafi, Muammar, 119

Gamsakhurdia, Zviad, 125

Gaprindashvili, Vazha, 234, 235

gas tariffs, 8

Gazprom, 3, 6, 8, 127, 129, 155, 174, 175–176, 177

GEC, 194

GEENTRANCE, 163–167

GEL (Georgian lari), 36, 37, 38, 42, 43, 44, 45–46, 47, 48, 71, 147, 189, 202–208. *See also* lari

Georgia

alternatives for in post-Communist era, 168–172

and EU membership, 106, 257–258

anti-crisis plan of, 246–247

aspirations of to join NATO, 33, 59, 106, 164

as attracted to Singapore, Dubai, and Hong Kong's experiences, 107

as energy resources transportation hub, 195

as losing hope and trust in West, NATO, and EU, 165

as not free of pro-Russian phenomenon, 232

as open to Russian capital, 20, 92

as part of Central Eurasia, 27, 28

as Russia's first target, 33, 59

as transit corridor, 140
decline in foreign investments in, 35–36
destabilization in, 236
economic growth of, 196, 216–220
executive power in, 11–12, 13, 14, 87, 89, 97
government as resembling authoritarianism more than democracy, 21
imports as outnumbering exports in, 36, 38, 44, 46, 141, 197, 200, 203–204, 219
inclusion of in SREB project, 192
international aid to, 45, 47, 79, 81–82, 93, 142–143, 197–198
investment of China in, 195
main trading partners of, 204
need for economists in, 209–214
new and mostly young and inexperienced government of, 10
parliamentary loyalty in, 11–12, 14
ranking in World Bank's *Doing Business*, 17, 89, 103, 104, 153
ranking on corruption of, 166, 170
Russian occupation of, 165, 235
Russia's interest in seeing pro-Russian political parties come to power in, 234
strengthening of American dollar in, 35, 38, 39, 82
success of in overcoming COVID-19 epidemic, 259
trade relations of with Russia, 146, 148, 204
"Georgia 2020," 180, 183, 185, 201, 211, 220
Georgian Dream (GD), 133, 135, 136, 144, 145, 173, 175, 176, 179, 180, 181, 188, 189, 190, 199, 214, 232, 233

Georgian Oil and Gas
Corporation, 174
Georgian Railway, 174
Georgia's Economist
(periodical), 209
GEP (Greater Eurasian
Partnership), 192–193
global economic crisis (2020),
241, 246
global financial crisis (2008),
35, 36, 40, 42, 44, 86,
94, 142–143, 242
globalization, COVID-19 and,
242, 243, 254–259
Gorbachev, Mikhail, 32–33, 57
"Governmental 4-Point Plan,"
181–185, 227
governmental "business," in
post-Soviet Georgia,
187–190
Great Silk Road, 191
Greater Central Asia, use of
term, 28
Greater Eurasian Partnership
(GEP), 192–193
Green Friday, 35–41, 46, 47,
81–83
Greenberg, Ruslan, 171, 172
gross domestic product (GDP),
139, 141, 143, 147, 153,
196, 216–219, 257

H

Happiness Index, 218
household appliances, import
of, 198
housing boom, 141
Hualing, 188
Human Development
Index, 218
human rights abuses, 18, 91,
103, 121, 132, 226
Hungary, ranking on
corruption of, 166
hydroelectric power, 130, 147

I

income tax rate, 74, 75,
182, 183
indebtedness, 80, 199, 219
Industrial Investors, 92. *See also*
Promyslennye investory
(Industrial Investors)
industrial sector, 257
industrialization, 201, 213, 220
inflation, 16, 38, 42, 43, 44,
45, 46, 69, 70, 71–72,
77, 78, 139, 185, 207,
242, 247–251
Inguri Power Plant, 4
initial public offering (IPO), of
Georgian Railway and

Georgian Oil and Gas
Corporation stakes, 174
INOGATE project, 192
Inter RAO, 130, 155
Interbank Currency Exchange
(ICE), 39, 46
Interbank Currency Market
(ICM), 81
internally displace persons
(IDPs), 43, 44
International Financial
Corporation, 103
International Monetary Fund
(IMF), 13, 16, 37, 45,
47, 55, 69, 70, 77, 81,
82, 83, 84, 90, 95, 105,
107, 156, 207, 225, 247
International Security
Assistance Force, 122
Ivanishvili, Bidzina, 124,
125–126, 127–128, 133,
135, 136, 144–145, 211,
232–233
Ivanov, Igor, 128

J

Jackson-Vanik amendment, 112
Joint Declaration of the
Warsaw Eastern
Partnership
Summit, 108

judiciary, loss of strength and
independence of, 14, 89,
121, 153

K

Kashagan oil field, 25
Kazakhstan
as founding member of
EAEU, 157, 159,
160, 165, 166,
169, 193
as part of Central Eurasia,
27, 28
corruption in, 166
Kazakhstan-Caspian
Transportation
System, 25
market reforms in, 159
Russia's interest in seeing
pro-Russian
political parties
come to power
in, 231
Kazakhstan-Caspian
Transportation
System, 25
Khudoni Power Plant, 4
Kitsmarishvili, Erosi, 95–96
knowledge-based economy,
183, 185, 201, 213, 220

Kosovo, West's recognition of, 7, 33, 34, 50–51, 52, 53, 58–59, 60

Kremlin sympathies, suspicion of, 124, 125–126, 127, 128

Krugman, Paul, 212, 223–224

Kutaisi
relocation of Parliament of Georgia to, 189
removal of Parliament of Georgia from, 190

Kvirikashvili, Giorgi, 174, 181, 188

Kyrgyzstan
and Free Economic Zone (FEZ), 161
as EAEU member, 157, 159, 165, 169, 193, 231
as part of Central Eurasia, 27, 28
corruption in, 166
market reforms in, 159
Russia's interest in seeing pro-Russian political parties come to power in, 231

L

labor code, 44, 47, 73–74, 89, 94, 95, 102–103, 107, 139, 155
labor relations, 74, 148
Lagarde, Christine, 225
lari, 35, 36, 37–38, 39, 40, 41, 42, 46, 71, 81, 82–83, 94, 202–208. *See also* GEL (Georgian lari)
Latvia, corruption in, 166
Lelo, 234
"liberal empire," doctrine of, 1–2, 3–4, 5–8, 91, 92, 129, 174
libertarian, defined, 152, 153, 154, 155, 156, 211, 226, 227
libertarianism, Georgian model of, 151–156, 211, 226, 227
live-on-TV arrests, 96–97

M

manufacturing sector, 141, 142
market competition, limitation of, 68–69
market economy, transition to, 139, 225
McCain, John, 134

media, control over, 14–15, 89, 132, 226
Medvedev, Dmitry, 56, 62
Melikishvili, Zurab, 40
Membership Action Plan (MAP), 164
Memorandum of Economic and Financial Policies for 2008–2009, 47, 94–95
Merabishvili, Ivane, 130
military readiness, 14
Minister of Defense/Ministry of Defense, responsibilities of, 15, 68, 105, 155
Minister of Energy, 176
Ministry of Agriculture, privatization of, building of, 188, 189
Ministry of Economic Development, responsibilities of, 15, 69
Ministry of Economy, privatization of building of, 188, 189, 190, 227
Ministry of Education and Science, poor condition of building of, 190
Ministry of Energy, Gazprom's talks with, 175, 176
Ministry of Foreign Affairs location of in emergency building, 190
privatization of building of, 189
relocation of, 189
Ministry of Internal Affairs, responsibilities of, 105, 154
Ministry of Justice, privatization of building of, 188, 189
Ministry of the Interior, responsibilities of, 15, 17, 68, 90
Moldova, gas cut off in, 3
Mubarak, Hosni, 119, 120
Multi-Plex, 67
munflation, 248–249

N

Nabucco gas project, 25
National Bank of Georgia (NBG), 36–37, 38, 39, 40, 45, 46, 69, 76–78, 81, 82, 198, 206, 207, 208
National Communications Commission, 67
national currency. *See* GEL (Georgian lari); lari;

Russian ruble (RUB);
Turkish lira (TRY)
national debt, 80
National Energy and Water
Supply Regulatory
Commission, 67
National Movement, 93, 122,
124, 127, 135, 155. *See
also* United National
Movement (UNM)
National Program on
Economic Growth and
Poverty Reduction, 83
NATO
cautionary approach of
toward Russia,
1, 166
challenges of, 259
Georgia's aspirations
to join, 33, 59,
106, 164
Georgia's intensive
cooperation with,
122, 163–164
Georgia's prospects of
joining, 7, 14,
19, 165
natural gas
percentage of that Europe
receives from
Russia, 33, 58
Russia's use of to exert
economic and
political pressure, 1,
5, 23–24, 175, 176
NBG (National Bank of
Georgia). *See* National
Bank of Georgia (NBG)
"near abroad," 5
neoliberal reforms, examples of,
103, 139
neoliberalism, 103, 104, 108,
139, 140
Noghaideli, Zurab, 95
noneconomic economic
policy, 222
noneconomic policy, 222–227
Norland, Richard, 135
North Caucasus, 24, 29, 130
Northern Caucasus, 28, 29
November 2007, events of,
9–10, 19, 21, 22, 86, 92

O

Obama, Barack, 126, 134, 135,
136, 165
OBOR initiative, 193
oil and gas revenues,
redistributive
mechanism of revenues
from, 159, 160, 177
Okruashvili, Irakli, 18, 95

Oliver-Tanzi Effect, 39
Orange Revolution, 6
ownership, principle of, 158–159

P

Parliament of Georgia
    as "government's notary," 14, 89
    relocation of, 189
    return to original location of, 190
Partnership for Peace project, 163–164
patrol police, 13, 87, 105
pensions, 10, 87, 246–251
"pipeline cold war," 24
"pipeline confrontation," 24
pipeline harmonization, 24–26
police brutality, 18
possession, principle of, 158–159
"Possessions in Exchange for Debt," 2
poverty level, 104, 139, 144, 147, 196–197
poverty reduction, 83–84
"price of liberty," 13, 88, 90, 105
primitivism, as trait of Georgia's modern economic policy, 179–186, 188, 227
private property
    improprieties against, 17
    redistribution of, 226–227
privatization, 14, 17, 65, 66, 67, 73, 88, 90, 92, 105–106, 188, 189, 190, 227
Promyslennye investory (Industrial Investors), 3
property rights
    disrespect for, 17
    infringement of/violation of, 65–66, 90, 97, 103, 106, 121, 132, 139, 153, 211, 226
protest rallies, 120, 151, 176
pro-Western image, 122
pro-Western sentiment, meaning of, 119
pseudo-libertarianism, 154, 156, 211
pseudo-Western status, 120, 122
public administration, as compared to business administration, 212
Public Choice theory, 224
public dissatisfaction, 197
public institutions, disruption of, 68

public property, sale of, 66–67, 90
Putin, Vladimir, 1, 57–58, 119, 126, 130, 233

R

RAO EES (Unified Energy Systems), 1, 2, 3–4, 6, 91
remittances from abroad, 36, 44, 141, 142, 197, 199
Risch, James, 135, 136
Road, 91
Romney, Mitt, 136
Rose Revolution, 2, 6, 9–10, 12, 14, 20, 22, 59, 65, 68, 79, 85, 86, 90, 92, 103, 104, 105, 106, 107, 121, 128, 129, 132, 133, 139, 141, 142, 152, 226, 233
rule of law, disrespect for, 14, 17, 89, 90
Russia
    anti-sanctions as imposed by, 161–162
    anti-Western stance of, 126
    aspirations of to join WTO, 111–112
    as banning import of Georgian agricultural products, 6–7, 114, 143, 154–155, 161
    as founding member of EAEU, 160, 169
    as recognizing Georgia's territorial integrity, 50
    revengefulness of, 58
    market reforms in, 159
    military aggression of, 45, 60, 62, 64, 93, 134
    military exercises in North Caucasus, 130
    model of economic modernization of, 193
    occupation of Georgia by, 165, 235
    quest of to restore semblance of old, shattered empire, 33
    scheme of to rehabilitate rail line, 4
    threats of expansion of in Caucasus, 173–178
    trade relations of with Georgia, 146, 148, 204

transferring Georgia's strategic facilities to, 233
Russian Railways, 174
Russian ruble (RUB), 204, 205
Russian-Georgian war (August 2008), 42, 43, 50, 57, 85, 86, 92, 93, 95, 110, 126–127, 142–143, 233

S

Saakashvili, Mikheil, 11, 12, 15, 18, 19, 20, 21–22, 59, 87, 92–93, 95, 96, 97, 107–108, 121, 122, 124, 125, 127, 128–129, 130, 132, 133, 134, 135–136, 140, 144, 149, 152, 154, 155, 210–211, 212, 214, 233, 236
Sarkozy, Nicolas, 62, 126–127, 217
savings, level of, 142
SCP (South Caucasus Pipeline), 24
SDS (State Department of Statistics), 15, 69–70
Sen, Amartya, 217
Serbia, as model of development for Georgia, 51, 52–53
Shaheen, Jeanne, 135, 136
Shevardnadze, Eduard, 2, 10, 12, 13, 19, 86–87, 125, 128–129, 164, 175, 210, 213
Shiller, Robert, 225
shock therapy, 226
Silk Road Economic Belt (SREB), 191, 192, 193, 194, 195
Silk Road Transport Corridor (SRTC) project, 192
Singapore, as example to Georgia, 107–108, 144, 155
Slovakia, corruption in, 166
social tax, 74, 75
"Social-Economic Development Strategy of Georgia—Georgia 2020," 180, 183, 185, 201, 211, 220
socioeconomic development, prospects for, 138–150, 201
South Caucasus
links of with West, 4
Russia's efforts to reorient, 2, 3, 4, 61
use of term, 29

South Caucasus Pipeline (SCP), 24
South Caucasus Railways, 174
South Ossetia
    annexation of by Russia, xviii, 20
    border monitors in, 113–114, 115–116
    independence of, 11
    Russia as recognizing independence of, 49, 50, 51, 59, 60, 61, 95, 110, 112, 127, 234
    Russian citizenship as granted to residents of, 7, 33, 34, 50, 60
    Russian military bases in, 49, 51, 95
    Russian troops in, 7
Southern Caucasus, 29
Special Industrial Zone, 76
SREB (Silk Road Economic Belt), 191, 192, 193, 194, 195
SRTC (Silk Road Transport Corridor) project, 192
Stability and Association Agreement (EU and Serbia), 52
Stanton Equities, 92
State Department of Statistics (SDS), 15, 69–70
statistics, role of in Georgia, 15–16, 69–70, 143, 248
"Statute of the Republic's High Economic Council," 213
Stiglitz, Joseph E., 207, 217, 224
strategic assets, disposal of Georgia's, 174
Sustainable Development of Georgia, 227
Switzerland
    as mediator in talks between Georgia and Russia, 112–113
    and tourism, 200

T

Tajikistan, as part of Central Eurasia, 27, 28
tax code, 139
tax policy, 184
tax rate, 74, 88. *See also* income tax rate; social tax
tax revenues, 12, 13, 38, 72, 73, 87, 156, 184
Tbilgaz, 66
Tengiz oil field, 25

tourism, 143, 147, 183, 188, 199–200, 203–204, 212–213, 219, 227
TRACECA project, 192
traffic police, 13, 87
Trans-Balkan Oil Pipeline, 25
Trans-Caspian pipeline, 25
Trans-Caucasus, 29
Trans-Caucasus Railway, 146
transit fee, 175, 176, 177
Transparency International, 166, 170
transportation sector, 147
Truman, Harry, 213
Trump, Donald, 165, 256
Turkey, as one of Georgia's main trading partners, 204–205
Turkish lira (TRY), 204, 205
Turkmenistan, as part of Central Eurasia, 27, 28
21st Century Maritime Silk Road, 191

U

UGDM (United Georgia Democratic Movement), 233, 234
UK, and tourism, 200
Ukraine
　and Georgian model of libertarianism, 151–156
　as one of Georgia's main trading partners, 204
　punishment of regarding gas prices, 6
　Russia's pressure on, 1, 5, 23–24, 236
unemployment allowances, 71
unemployment levels, 143
UNICEF, 197
Unified Energy Systems (RAO EES), 1, 2, 3–4, 6, 91
Unified Machinery Plants ("Ob'yedinionnye mashostroitel'nye zavody"), 152
United Bank of Georgia, 66–67
United Georgia Democratic Movement (UGDM), 233, 234
"United Georgia without Poverty!," 83
United Georgian Bank, 3, 92, 129
United Heavy Engineering Group OMZ, 129

United National Movement
(UNM), 174, 175, 183,
184, 188, 189, 190, 198,
199, 226, 232, 233. *See
also* National Movement
United States
and tourism, 200
as fostering South Caucasus's
links with West, 4
as support of Georgia's
independent
statehood, 165
economic sanctions against
Russia by, 161
intervention of to rehabilitate
pipeline, 3, 6
Jackson-Vanik amendment, 112
presidential election (2008),
133, 134
role of in enabling return of
aggressive nationalism in
Russia, 33
role of in encouraging Georgia
to get closer to EU,
54–55
Saakashviki as proving
devotion to, 122
United States–Georgia Charter
on Strategic Partnership,
140, 146, 148

universities, national
examinations for
admission to, 13, 88
Uzbekistan, as part of Central
Eurasia, 27, 28

V

Vashadze, Grigol, 232
Vietnam, Russian agreement
with, 160
Vneshtorgbank (VTB), 3,
66–67, 92, 129, 155
"voluntary contributions" from
businesses, 16, 105

W

West
as turning blind eye
to Russia's
antidemocratic
actions, 57–58
as turning blind eye
to Saakashvili
government's
failures, 19–20
calls from for
strengthening
democracy, 119, 120
democracy as more of
stated commitment
than real goal, 120

  double standard of for
    democracy, 21
  Georgia as new testing
    ground for, 122
  reluctance of to recognize
    Abkhazia and South
    Ossetia, 34
  Russia's turn to in late
    1980s and early
    1990s, 57
White Stream gas project, 25
World Bank, 17, 45, 55, 83, 84, 89, 93, 103, 107, 147, 153, 156, 196
World Health Organization, 255
World Trade Organization (WTO), 109, 110, 111, 112, 114–115, 116, 146, 148, 194

Y

Yanukovych, Victor, 6
Yeltsin, Boris, 2, 32–33, 57

CPSIA information can be obtained
at www.ICGtesting.com
Printed in the USA
BVHW071844270121
598861BV00003B/229

9 781663 207623